On My Terms

KARIN SHAM POO

authorHOUSE®

AuthorHouse™
1663 Liberty Drive
Bloomington, IN 47403
www.authorhouse.com
Phone: 1 (800) 839-8640

Published by AuthorHouse 07/25/2018

ISBN: 978-1-5462-5240-5 (sc)
ISBN: 978-1-5462-5238-2 (hc)
ISBN: 978-1-5462-5239-9 (e)

Library of Congress Control Number: 2018908670

To my daughter, Elizabeth, and my granddaughter, Sonja.
This book is for you.
Without you, this book would not have been written.

1

The Phone Call That Changed My Life

In April 1985, I was at a hotel outside Oslo while attending a planning meeting with senior colleagues at Christiania Bank, where I was senior vice president. During a break, one of the hotel receptionists told me that I urgently had to call my assistant. I wondered what could be that urgent but decided, of course, to call.

My assistant told me that she had received a call from an ambassador in the Ministry of Foreign Affairs. He wanted to talk to me, and I needed to call him immediately. *How strange*, I thought. *What does he want?*

"What do you know about UNICEF?" he asked after I called him.

"Not too much," I replied. "I know it's a part of the UN that deals with children. I know that one can buy UNICEF cards. That is more or less all."

His next question stopped me in my tracks: "Would you be interested in being a candidate for the position of comptroller—finance director—at UNICEF?"

He told me there would be other candidates from other countries, but he knew that UNICEF was looking for more women in senior positions and that Norway—one of the largest contributors—was quite underrepresented. Because he knew I was one of the few women in senior banking positions in Norway—I had been the country's first female senior vice president when I'd been appointed to the position three years earlier—he had easily tracked me down. He gave me three days to think about whether or not I would be a candidate. I had a great job that I truly enjoyed, and I had no plans to leave. Furthermore, I had never entertained the thought of going abroad. But there was no doubt that it sounded tempting.

This was before the internet and Google, so what I could find out about UNICEF in such a short time was limited to a few papers the ambassador from the ministry kindly delivered to my office on foot.

My daughter, Elizabeth, was already in college in California, and my first marriage had not been doing well for some time, so I decided that the first person I'd consult would be my father. As always, he came up with a lot of questions and advice, including pointing out that nothing might come of it—and even if it did, I could always say no.

After three days of much back and forth, I informed the Ministry of Foreign Affairs that I would accept the candidacy.

A couple of weeks later, I received a phone call from the director of human resources at UNICEF in New York. He told me that he was going to interview several candidates and wanted to come to Oslo to interview me the following week. I was not sure what to expect, but the interview turned out to be straightforward. From my point of view, it went well.

Two weeks passed. Then the call came from UNICEF in New York. Could I come for an interview next week? I said yes. At that stage, I had to tell my boss; I could not just go to New York without telling him. I called and asked to see him on an important issue. As always, he easily found time for me. I told him what was at stake and asked him to keep my candidacy between the two of us for the time being. He was excited and supportive and told me that both Norway and Christiania Bank would be proud if I were to be selected.

So there I was, going to New York. I had been there before on business, but this time would be a whirlwind interview trip. I would arrive in the early afternoon, have a full day of interviews, and then have a couple of more interviews the next morning before heading to the airport to return to Oslo.

I have always had an excellent memory. However, my memory of the interviews—and there were twelve of them in a day and a half—is faint. What I do remember very well are all the people I met. They were fascinating and interesting people in different ways. One of the interviews was with Jim Grant, the executive director of UNICEF. I still remember his firm handshake, his steel blue eyes, and his charisma. Like all the others, he asked a lot of questions that I tried to answer as well as I could. He told me there were five additional candidates for the position. Two of them had been interviewed already, and the last two were expected to interview shortly.

On my way back from the UNICEF office, I passed a new apartment building on the corner of Second Avenue and Forty-Ninth Street. The building had a sign with apartments for rent and a phone number. I did not go in, but I wrote down the phone number just in case.

Around three weeks later, I was again in New York, this time as a speaker at a banking conference. As I had promised the last time I'd been in New York, I contacted the counselor at the Norwegian Permanent Mission to the UN. We had a wonderful dinner together; it was the first time I tasted soft-shell crabs, which I came to love. She told me that she'd heard that UNICEF expected to make a decision shortly, and she had also heard that I was one of the leading candidates.

Back in Oslo, I decided to do some more detailed planning. I had discussions with my boss, who was one of the executive vice presidents of Christiania Bank. Since I was planning to return to the bank after two to four years in New York, I needed to find out whether the bank would give me a leave of absence. At this stage, it was necessary to bring the bank's president into the picture. After a couple of days, the executive vice president informed me that top management would be happy to give me a two-year leave of absence, and if I would like to stay on for another two years, they would extend the leave of absence accordingly. They really wanted me back. He also said that top management would be proud to have one of its senior staff members in a position like this at the UN. I was more touched than I managed to express.

In early June, the phone call came. Jim Grant himself was on the phone to tell me that the job was mine. He wanted me to join as soon as possible, preferably mid-July. Since I had had some time to think about it, I told him I was pleased and honored to accept the position of comptroller for a two-year period. I needed, however, some time to wrap up my work and would be able to join on September 1. While he had hoped I would join earlier, he understood. Faxes and big envelopes arrived from UNICEF over the next few weeks with my appointment letters, papers to get the necessary visa from the US Embassy in Oslo, forms for my medical checkup, etc. The ball was rolling fast.

I decided to call the office of the apartment building I had seen in New York to inquire whether it had any one-bedroom apartments for rent. I got the clear impression that the office had never before rented an apartment to a person sight unseen, but the staff members were very helpful. They faxed me the floor plan of a vacant one-bedroom on the fifteenth floor, the lease agreement, and other relevant papers. I agreed to rent it from September 1 and sent them the necessary deposit and the first month's rent.

I was going to ship some furniture from Oslo but needed a bed, bookshelf, dining table, and chairs. A colleague in Christiania Bank told me that he knew a person who owned a furniture store in New York and offered to ask him to call me. He did, and I placed the order of what I needed. I then called the rental office of the apartment building and asked if it was okay to have the furniture delivered to the apartment a few days before my arrival. Again, they were accommodating. I also made the necessary arrangements for electricity and phone. My plan was to stay only one night at a hotel and then move into the apartment on September 1, which was Labor Day. I would start work on September 2.

So on August 31, 1985, I left Oslo for New York. Little did I know at the time that I would never (at least so far) come back on a permanent basis. My biggest surprise, which I found so touching, was that even though I had said goodbye to my parents the day before, my mother was at the airport to see me off.

Everything went as I had planned. I moved into the apartment September 1. While it would still take some weeks for the shipment from Oslo to arrive, the furniture I had ordered was there. After spending the rest of the day doing necessary shopping, I could function.

The next day, I went to the office early. The first person I met was my assistant, June, who was wonderful. She had arrived early to make sure she was there when I arrived. We briefly discussed how I would like to spend my first week. She assumed I wanted to take some time off to look for an apartment. She almost fell off her chair when I told her that I already had one and that I had actually moved in the day before. She had arranged for a staff meeting so I could meet with all the staff in the afternoon. I already knew from the briefing material that I had eighty-five staff members from

4

more than thirty countries. In addition to an all-staff meeting, I asked June to arrange for meetings with all staff members on a one-to-one basis over the next few weeks and to set aside thirty minutes for each staff member. I had a deputy comptroller whom I wanted, of course, to meet with first. I also wanted to meet with the previous comptroller again (I had met with him while in New York for interviews a few months earlier). A great Italian man, he was presently doing some important work for UNICEF on a consultancy basis to create specific financial rules and regulations for UNICEF. The meetings with individual staff members were a great success. It took me around a month to finish all of them, but this was a good investment of time. It gave me an excellent opportunity to get to know the staff and for them to get to know me.

In addition to my staff meetings, arrangements had also been made for me to meet with all the other directors and senior staff—a few of whom I had met during my interviews for the position. This included the deputy executive director I was reporting to, who happened to be Swedish. It was both exciting and challenging to meet so many people from all over the world. English was spoken with so many different accents, which was both an advantage and a disadvantage. I did not have to worry about my Norwegian accent when I spoke, but this also made it almost impossible to get rid of it.

I learned quickly that I was the only woman at the director level at the UNICEF headquarters in New York. However, the Division of Human Resources (called Division of Personnel at that time) had a few months earlier filled its deputy director post with a woman. Outside of New York, there were two regional directors who were women—one for Latin America and the Caribbean and one for the region of eastern and southern Africa.

In 1985, women filled only 25 percent of professional positions at UNICEF worldwide. Coming from the banking sector in Norway, which was a very male-dominated sector, particularly at senior level, this was not new for me. However, I was thrilled to learn that the executive director had established a task force earlier in 1985 to come up with recommendations on how to improve the percentage of women in professional posts in UNICEF. Based on these recommendations, the executive director had set a goal that most people felt was very ambitious—an increase to 40 percent by 1990.

I had been fighting for gender equality since my late teens. I had worked hard to get more women in management and middle management positions in the banks I had worked at, and I had been a speaker on these issues at various meetings and conferences in Norway on several occasions. I was excited to work for an organization whose executive director was willing to focus on and set clear goals for women in the workforce.

After reading, talking to people, and learning more and more about UNICEF's finances, I discovered that the organization had a number of financial challenges in addition to all the other challenges typical for an organization like UNICEF. The total contributions to UNICEF in 1985 amounted to $362 million. Administrative costs accounted for $39 million; the rest went to program support or direct program expenditures. Country offices were allocated funds for executive-board-approved programs every year. In the past, many offices had not spent their full allocations. To try to speed up spending, over the last few years, including in 1985, offices had been allocated around 125 percent of their normal allocation. That worked well for a while, drawing on accumulated cash reserve, but in 1985 this started to become a problem. I could see that we ran the risk of spending more funds than we had. I alerted my boss, the deputy executive director, who suggested I see Jim Grant to discuss this challenge and my recommendation for how to deal with it.

So there I was, after two months in UNICEF, in the executive director's office with news I knew he would not like to hear—but I had no choice. After I explained the situation, he looked at me intensely and asked what I would suggest we do. I was prepared for that. I had a recommendation for how to resolve the situation in the short term as well as what to change so we did not find ourselves in the same situation again. For the rest of the year, we asked the largest country offices to slow down on expenditures, including filling vacant positions. When we closed the books for 1985, the total expenditures were $377 million—$15 million more than our income. We had used all the accumulated reserve, but it could have been worse if we had not taken action. Future allocations to country offices would be monitored carefully to avoid poor implementation or a level of expenditures we could not afford.

In 1985, around 50 percent of all of UNICEF's expenditures were direct supply assistance to our various programs in developing countries. The supply consisted of everything from vaccines and essential drugs to water pumps and pipes—and everything in between. The government of Denmark had built a large warehouse facility at the port in Copenhagen for UNICEF. The management and its director were, however, in New York at the time. The facilities in Copenhagen were to be expanded, and most of the supply operation was to be consolidated to Copenhagen, leaving only a small office in New York. Because of its financial and program importance, my first travel for UNICEF was to Copenhagen. I experienced how items were picked, assembled, packed, and shipped. The warehouse was impressive and very well organized. It is important to remember that this was before operations became heavily computerized and automated.

Living in New York was also exciting. I had been to New York a few times on business trips while working in banking, but I never really liked the city. I had preferred places like San Francisco, where I found people much friendlier. But here I was, living in New York City, and I had to make the best of it. I fast learned that walking was a good way to get around and to learn the city. I had figured out that on average, each street took one minute and each avenue took three minutes when walking. That was a good way to calculate how long it would take to walk from point A to point B. I enjoyed walking in Central Park on Sundays when the weather was nice. I visited Saint Patrick's Cathedral, which I found beautiful and impressive, and I also found the Norwegian Seamen's Church on Forty-Ninth Street, close to where I lived. I would later become deeply involved with the Norwegian Seamen's Church as a treasurer and board member for sixteen years.

When I did not walk, I would often take a taxi to get around. Taxis are easy to get in New York; you just stand on the corner, look for a taxi, and stretch your arm out for the taxi to hopefully stop. Busses were also easy, but the subway, which was used by thousands every day, never became my favorite. I did use it from time to time, particularly for going with friends to Chinatown, which was and still is an exciting place in New York.

I had eaten Chinese food before New York. In fact, that was the first type of foreign food restaurant to open in Norway when a Chinese place opened in Oslo in 1963. (Today you can get food from any part of the world in Oslo.) I went with a girlfriend there for dinner just after they opened in 1963, and we found the food exotic and tasty. I discovered later that food there was very much adjusted to please the Norwegian palate. I had also enjoyed excellent Chinese food in Chinatown in San Francisco when I was there in 1983. However, dim sum in Chinatown in New York on Sundays with friends was a new experience that I liked very much.

While I had started to get a good grip on UNICEF's finances, I realized fast that the only way to understand what UNICEF was all about was to visit its field offices. Comptrollers before me had not really done this, but everybody thought it was a smart idea. So where to start? I had traveled to Europe, North Africa, and the United States before I joined UNICEF. The part of the world I knew least about, however, was Latin America and the Caribbean. So after consultation with a number of people, I decided that my first trip would be to that region. What I did not know then was that destiny would have me become intimately attached to that region a few years later.

The UNICEF regional office for Latin America and the Caribbean wanted me to visit one of the two countries in the region with the highest child mortality, Bolivia or Haiti. These were also the poorest countries in the region. The trip would take place in February 1986. The regional office had originally decided that I would visit Haiti, but with increasing unrest in that country late in 1985, they decided I would visit Bolivia instead. That was a wise decision; the unrest in Haiti increased, and in February 1986 the president, Jean-Claude Duvalier (known as Baby Doc), and his family were ousted from the country. All UN international staff were also evacuated for a period of time. The ousting of Duvalier started a shaky transition to democratic rule in Haiti.

Before traveling to Bolivia, I moved into another apartment. While I liked the apartment on Forty-Ninth Street, it had been a short-term lease, and I wanted something more permanent. After looking around I found another brand-new apartment in a nice rental building on Thirty-Fourth Street between First Avenue and the East River. It was on the twenty-ninth floor and somewhat bigger than my first place. It had a balcony facing First Avenue and a real window in the kitchen, which is rather rare in apartments in Manhattan. From the window I had a view of the boats and barges that made their way up and down the East River.

Even though it has been more than twenty-nine years since my trip to Bolivia, I am surprised by how many details of that trip I still remember. As I have mentioned, Bolivia was one of the two poorest countries in Latin America and the Caribbean, and it had one of the two highest child mortality rates in 1986. With a population of 6 million, the life expectancy was fifty-one years. The gross national product per capita was $510, and the child mortality rate was 195 per thousand. That meant that 19.5 percent of children died before their fifth birthday.

I left for Bolivia early in February 1986. I was excited about the trip. I went first to Miami, where I changed planes to head off to El Alto airport, which was just outside the capital of La Paz. I had been warned about the altitude. La Paz is the highest national capital in the world, and the airport itself is at the highest part of La Paz, 13,313 feet above sea level. I had been told that some suffer from altitude sickness the first days after arrival. After I arrived, I learned that the office had brought an oxygen tank, just in case. I felt fine and continued to feel fine throughout the trip. Upon my arrival at the hotel, they gave me a thermos of tea that was supposed to help prevent altitude sickness. The tea was coca tea (also called *mate de coca*) made from raw leaves of the coca plant that were steeped in hot water. The coca tea was and is legal in Bolivia, Peru, Colombia, and Ecuador but is now somewhat discouraged. The leaves, when extracted chemically, are the source for cocaine. However, the raw leaves used in the tea have only a slight coca alkaloid. I drank a cup of the tea every day throughout my stay in Bolivia; since I felt fine, it may have helped!

The program was light the first couple of days. Despite my assurances, they were concerned that I would feel exhausted. They must have had bad experiences with other visitors in the past.

First I went to the office and met with all the staff. I also met with ministers and other government officials. It turned out that everybody was excited about my visit. While they had had visits from the regional office, they had never had a visit by a senior staff member from New York. My title—comptroller (in Spanish, *la controlora*)—had created some concern. They were not sure what I wanted to check and whether any of the programs were in jeopardy, but they were soon assured that was not the purpose of my visit.

The government had embarked on a number of measures to reduce the child mortality rate, with the support of UNICEF and others. They had started vaccination campaigns, school feedings, and adding iodine to salt to combat the high incidence of goiter—65 percent of schoolchildren had goiter—just to mention a few initiatives. They had also just started a fascinating measure aimed at reducing mortality and improving development among prematurely born babies. It was called "The Mother Kangaroo Method" and had made its Bolivian debut in the San Gabriel Hospital in La Paz, which I visited.

The Mother Kangaroo Method was first developed in the Instituto Materno Infantil in Bogota, Colombia, in 1979. Due to increasing morbidity and mortality, they had decided to introduce a method to alleviate the shortage of caregivers and lack of resources. It was suggested that mothers had continuous skin-to-skin contact with their babies who had low birth weight. This would keep them warm. They were also to exclusively breastfeed, as possible. The babies were also discharged earlier, lowering the risk of infections and lower respiratory tract diseases. All of this had improved the survival rate for premature babies and babies with low birth weight. UNICEF supported this method from the start.

To see these tiny babies—many of them around two pounds—carried around by their mothers close to their chests was amazing. The mothers I spoke with felt very comfortable with the method.

My visit to Bolivia also included a trip to Oruro, which was around a three-hour drive south of La Paz. I was up for a big treat—Carnival in Oruro. I had heard and read about Carnival or Mardi Gras in France, Italy, and Brazil, but my knowledge was limited. And what is so interesting is that just a few years after my visit to Oruro, Carnival—albeit in another country—became an important annual event in my life.

I was told that Carnival in Oruro dated back more than two thousand years. Originally an indigenous festival, it was later transformed to incorporate Christian aspects.

It was colorful and fascinating—I had never seen anything like it in my entire life. There were more than a hundred bands with several thousand participants and musicians. One of the performances revolved around the classic battle between good and evil and was called Dance de Diablada—the Devil Dance.

I have always felt that things happen for a reason. There was a reason that my first UNICEF travel was to the Latin American and Caribbean region and that I was taken to Oruro to see Carnival. It was a way to prepare me for what was ahead in my life.

The programs that UNICEF supported in the Oruro district were integrated community-based programs in health, water and sanitation, nutrition, education, and income generation. They wanted to inaugurate two health clinics and a water well that had been built with UNICEF's support. In accordance with Oruro tradition, I was given a bottle of locally brewed beer and asked to shake it, open it, and sprinkle it around the building I inaugurated. Having done that a few times, my clothes and my skin smelled like beer. I remember how good it felt to wash it away in the shower that night.

The income-generation and nutrition projects were interesting as well. Breeding guinea pigs, who multiply fast, provided locals with a great source of protein. I had the opportunity to taste guinea pig during lunch; it tasted a bit like rabbit.

Back in La Paz, I was told that the UNICEF staff had arranged for a boat trip on Lake Titicaca the next day, a Sunday that would be my last day in Bolivia. Lake Titicaca is on the border of Bolivia and Peru and is one of the largest lakes in Latin America. It was a beautiful and clear day, and I saw a lot of water birds. But I was up for an unexpected treat in addition to the beautiful nature I enjoyed. I was told that Lake Titicaca was known for the locals' reed boats, which are made from a special reed that grows around the lake. This reed has been used for boats for a few thousand years. That caught my attention immediately: the Norwegian ethnographer and adventurer Thor Heyerdahl had had his second reed boat, *Ra II*, built by reed-boat builders from Lake Titicaca. He and his crew sailed this reed boat successfully from Morocco to Barbados to demonstrate that the ancient Mediterranean or African people could have crossed the Atlantic and reached the Americas in reed boats. I saw several reed boats of different sizes, and then we went ashore to meet some of the boatbuilders. One of them got excited when he heard I was from Norway. He told me that he was one of the four boatbuilders who had built *Ra II* and that he had been to Oslo, Norway, and, together with Thor Heyerdahl, had met the Norwegian king, Olav V, in 1980. He gave me a small replica of a reed boat, which I later gave to my father when I went to see him in Oslo a few months later.

From Bolivia I went to UNICEF's regional office for Latin America and the Caribbean in Bogota, Colombia. On a quarterly basis the regional office hosted a meeting with all the UNICEF representatives' heading offices in the region to discuss and make decisions on region-specific issues. I had been looking forward to meeting one of the two women regional directors in UNICEF. With the support of UNICEF, many countries in the region were in the forefront of implementing programs to reduce child deaths and improve the health of children through massive vaccination programs against preventable childhood diseases, the use of oral rehydration salt to combat dehydration in connection with diarrhea, and the promotion of breastfeeding; these programs would gradually be implemented globally with UNICEF support.

In Bogota I met the deputy regional director, Fritz, who had arranged my trip to Bolivia, for the first time. I easily become friendly with people, but that does not mean that I will become close friends with everyone I meet. With Fritz it was different. We liked each other from the first time we met. He'd had extensive UNICEF experience in different parts of the world before he'd been appointed deputy regional director for Latin America and the Caribbean. He took his job seriously, worked extremely hard, and was a great support to the regional director—a good example of a good team. But Fritz also liked and still likes nice music, dance, and good food, and he is a talented cook. Thirty-two years later, Fritz and I are still close friends, and he and my husband also became good friends the first time they met. We have visited him in Montreal, where he lives when he is not doing consultancies for the UN, and he has stayed with us in New York and for long periods in Trinidad while he had consultancies as head of the regional support center for UNAIDS in the Caribbean.

Back in New York, I reflected on my experiences over the previous two weeks. In addition to having met a number of fantastic and interesting people, the trip had given me a much clearer picture of what UNICEF was all about and what could be done to improve the situation of children in the world.

In April 1986, I experienced my first UNICEF Executive Board meeting. While I had a lot of experience with board meetings in the banks I had worked for and from other organizations with which I had been involved, this was very different. The board consisted of representatives from forty-one member states of the UN, each elected for three years at a time on a regional rotating basis. And each of the member states attended not with one person but with a delegation of several people. In addition, any member states of the UN that were not represented at the board could attend as observers. That meant that around two hundred people would attend. The UNICEF Executive Board meeting took place once a year back then and lasted for two weeks. This would later change and become more streamlined with three shorter meetings. UNICEF celebrated its fortieth anniversary in 1986, and I can still hear Jim Grant's forceful voice in his opening statement declaring that UNICEF's goal was to have a world full of bright, happy, alert, and joyful children.

While my first board meeting was both overwhelming and a little bit confusing, I fast learned the ropes so I could know what to do and say and how the board functioned. I would play many important roles in board meetings and be instrumental in getting board decisions through over the next nineteen years.

When the deputy executive director was traveling, I would act for him unless I was traveling myself. That meant that I quickly gained a good insight into many areas of UNICEF's work over and above my responsibilities. In the early part of 1987, the deputy executive director, my boss, asked for study leave. He also indicated that he would prefer to do something else, preferably outside New York, when the study leave ended. At that point, I was asked to be the acting deputy executive director on a longer term basis. In the fall of 1987, the position as regional director for South Asia had become vacant, and Karl Eric Knutsson informed Jim Grant that even though it was a position at a director level, he would be much happier and felt he could contribute more as regional director. Jim Grant then appointed him to that position and, at the same time, informed me that he would recommend to the UN secretary general, Perez de Cuellar, that I be appointed to the position of deputy executive director of operations of UNICEF. Positions at that level had to be approved by the UN secretary general. On December 1, 1987, the appointment letter came.

I was appointed deputy executive director of UNICEF at the assistant secretary general level. I was a few weeks short of forty-four years old and the only woman at that level in the UN system at the time. I felt that it was the right time to reflect on how I had managed to get so far.

2

Early Years

I was born on a Saturday—December 18, 1943, at 5:15 p.m., in Oslo, Norway, in the maternity ward at the Women's Hospital. It was in the middle of World War II, and Norway had been occupied by Nazi Germany since April 9, 1940.

When I was small, my father frequently told me I was born with a big bang. When I got a little older, he told me more details. On December 19, 1943, some hours after I was born, a big explosion took place down by the waterfront while dockworkers were unloading a lot of ammunition from a German ship. Many people, both Germans and Norwegians, were killed and injured, and several hundred buildings were severely damaged. The fires and explosions lasted late into the night. My mother told me that all the babies were brought to their mothers and wheeled down to the basement for shelter. This must have been terrifying for somebody who had just had her first baby. My father told me how he'd desperately tried to get to the hospital. He wore a pair of galoshes over his regular shoes because of the snow, and they were full of holes from the shrapnel that was spread all over the city. Whether this explosion was sabotage or not never became clear.

My parents had bought a children's journal when I was born, and they entered important data and information about my first few years there. From the journal I know that in addition to my father, my two grandmothers and three of my aunts visited us in the hospital. We left the hospital on Christmas Eve in a taxi with my aunt Kilda, my father's oldest sister, and went to my paternal grandmother's apartment, where we spent Christmas Eve.

My parents, Ruth and Thomas, got married in October 1942, a year or so before I was born. They were both twenty-eight when I was born and had known each other for a number of years before they got married. My mother actually was friendly with my father's youngest sister, my aunt Marie, before she knew my father well. Since none of them belonged to what was until recently the State Church, they got married in a civil ceremony. However, the wedding reception took place on the premises of the Church of Christ in Oslo, an Evangelical Lutheran Free Church that my maternal grandmother and my late grandfather belonged to and where my mother went to Sunday school and was confirmed as a child. Because of the War and its required rationing, it was not easy to get enough meat for the wedding reception, but apparently a number of people helped with their rationing cards. They managed, among other things, to buy a five-pound can of corned beef, which became one of the ingredients for a beef stew (even though some of it almost disintegrated during the cooking). I was told that it did, however, taste good.

My father was the assistant janitor for a tenement apartment building on the east side of Oslo where he and his family had lived since 1917, when he was around two years old. The building was built around a cobblestone courtyard, and only the apartments in the front part of the complex had windows facing the street. The rest had windows facing the courtyard and were, of course, much darker. At the end of the courtyard were the latrines, a two-floor construction with eight latrines on each floor. While all the apartments had water, none of them had a toilet. The latrines were emptied regularly, but they still smelled, and rats scurried around. I never liked to go there, but of course I had to when I got older.

On the ground floor facing the street were two stores on each side of the gate—one was a shop where my mother sold cigarettes, sweets, and newspapers, and the other was a bakery where my aunt Marie worked.

My mother and father lost their fathers the same year, in 1935. My paternal grandfather was born in Vordingborg, Denmark. He was seventy-six when he died and had been ailing for quite a while, so his passing was not unexpected. With my maternal grandfather, it was very different. He was fifty-eight and in good shape when he suddenly took ill with meningitis and passed away after a few days. This was a big shock to my grandmother, my mother, and all her siblings. My father and his family had had another death in the family just a few months before his father passed away. His only brother, Andreas, had passed away from tuberculosis, which unfortunately was a common cause of death at that time among relatively young people. Uncle Andreas was only twenty-one when he passed away.

While my father grew up in the city, my mother and her siblings grew up in a house southeast of Oslo. My grandfather was a master carpenter and built the house where my mother and her siblings grew up.

While my mother had rented a room from one of the tenants in the building complex where she worked, she would normally go home to my grandmother on Saturday after work and stay there until Sunday afternoon. One Saturday night, on her way home, a car hit her. Thankfully the accident was not too serious, but one of her knees was damaged. She was confined to mostly sitting in a chair with her leg elevated for six weeks. During that period, my father, who had been dating my mother for a while, walked all the way to visit her every Sunday. I would guess it took close to two hours to walk uphill to the house. My mother, and no doubt my grandmother too, were impressed. When my mother was well enough to get back to work, she accepted his proposal to marry him.

After my grandfather died so unexpectedly, my grandmother found it more and more difficult to keep the house. Except for my aunt Marit, all her other children had either already moved out or were in the process of doing so, so when with the help of my father, my maternal grandmother and my aunt were able to rent an apartment in the same tenement complex where my paternal grandmother lived. Others in the family lived there too. One of my maternal grandfather's sisters, Gunda, married my maternal grandmother's half-brother, Mazelius, when she was around fifty-five. She had never been married before, but he had been; he had grown children. They rented an apartment in the front part of the tenement complex that faced the street. These were the largest apartments. And to make the story complete, my aunt Marie, my father's youngest sister, married a widower named Reinhardt when I was around two and a half years old. Uncle Reinhardt, as he then became, had a son named Tor, who was exactly my age; I have always considered him my cousin. They also lived in the same complex and on the same floor as Aunt Gunda and Uncle Mazelius. So when I was small, one of my grandmothers or one of my aunts could just walk me from one grandmother or aunt to another, and when I was a little older, I could do it by myself.

I was not born into a family with a lot of material wealth. I was, however, fortunate to be born into a family with a lot of love and care. As the firstborn of my generation, I got a lot of extra attention and love, which had an important and positive impact on my development.

My parents both had new jobs when they got married. My father worked in a printing office where he would remain over the next thirty years, and my mother had started to clean the offices of a publishing house three times a week at night.

It was not easy to get their own place to live, but they had managed to rent a small cottage on the premises of somebody my maternal grandmother knew. We lived there until I was around a year old. I do not remember what the place was like, but my mother told me it was like a large a dollhouse. It was a nice and quiet neighborhood, beautiful in the spring and summer. Unfortunately, during the winter it became very damp, which was not good for any of us—particularly not for me. I got bronchitis before I was one year old, which would continue to plague me every winter until I was in my late teens. It still sometimes comes back even today if I get a bad cold.

I was christened on May 14, 1944, in the neighborhood church and then officially was given the names Karin Elise after my two grandmothers. My mother had wanted to call me Eva, but my two grandmothers apparently insisted that I be named after them.

My parents realized that it would not be good to continue to live in the cottage, but it was difficult to find another place. Norway was still occupied by the Nazi Germans, no new apartments and houses were being built. Furthermore, many people, particularly from the Northern parts of Norway that had been burned and bombed severely, had moved south to the Oslo area, which made it even more difficult.

One of my father's cousins, Arnt, who was educated as a printer, and his wife, Margot, lived in a small apartment on the west side of Oslo, close to the royal castle. In the fall of 1944, they had a daughter, Reidun. Uncle Arnt and Auntie Margot, as I called them, were not happy living in Oslo, even though Uncle Arnt had a relatively good job. They missed Fie, the small fishing village in the southern part of Norway where my paternal grandmother was from and where they had both grown up. Taking a chance on the indications that the War would soon be over, he gave up his job, and they moved back to Fie. The family still had land there, so as soon as the War was over and they were able to get the necessary permits, they built a nice house by the water. Uncle Arnt became one of the best mackerel fishermen in the area, and together with his older brother, Uncle Sigvart, who was also a fisherman, he bought a shrimp trawler and was successful in shrimp fishing as well.

My mother and father were also lucky to find and rent a small apartment then, and we moved in early 1945.

The apartment was around 350 square feet and was on the ground floor of a two-story building. The apartment complex consisted of two buildings, a four-story building in the front and the two-story building in the back. There was a separate entrance to the apartment from the backyard. The entrance was small, with two doors, one of which led to the bathroom and the other to the living room. The bathroom had a toilet and a sink with only cold water; this was the only water source in the apartment. The living room was the main part of the apartment. We had a sofa, coffee table, and two chairs. The sofa was a sleep sofa, where my parents slept. We had a dining table with eight chairs, which is where we ate most of our meals, and in the corner was my bed with a folding screen around it. Then there was the kitchenette with a stove; we stored all our kitchen supplies on shelves. My father made a narrow folding table where he and my mother often had tea and sandwiches when she got back from work at night.

When I was small, my mother would bathe me once a week in a zinc tub she would move from the bathroom into the middle of the living room. It was a long process, since water first had to be heated on the stove and then mixed with cold water for the right temperature. From when I was around five, my mother would bring me to a public bath that was a five-minute walk from where we lived. I loved using the showers and then drying my hair afterward. I was not allowed to use the sauna until I got older, but from an early age I could use the shallow end of the swimming pool. I had learned to swim at an early age, so it wasn't long before I could use the whole pool.

A tall black cast-iron oven where one could burn either coke (a porous kind of coal) or wood heated the apartment. When my younger brother, Hans, was small, he found the oven frightening. I liked it, however. When my mother polished it every summer and it became black and shiny, I thought it looked even nicer.

The apartment had stained windows high up toward the ceiling that faced the backyard and also big windows on the other side of the apartment that faced a garden with two big cherry trees. The owners of this part of the apartment complex ran a boarding house and lived in a part of the house. They had two sons, Stein, who was four years older than I was, and Thor, who was born the year after we moved in. The only other tenant in this part of the apartment complex was the janitor for the entire complex. He lived there with his wife and two daughters, who must have been in their late teens when we moved in.

Boarding houses in apartment complexes had been common in Oslo for around one hundred years, and a number of them could be found in this part of the city as well as in neighborhoods catering to more well-to-do tenants. In the front building of the apartment complex, there were two boarding houses. They both catered to unmarried women who had come to Oslo to work, and these women all had good jobs—some working in the postal service, others as secretaries in private companies, and after the War was over, many worked in local and central government ministries.

On May 8, 1945, the Germans surrendered unconditionally, which took effect in Norway at midnight on May 9. The ceremonial surrender took place at Akershus Castle on May 11, 1945, and one can still find a picture of the occasion in many Norwegian homes. The king and crown prince of Norway and the Norwegian government had been in exile in London since Norway had been occupied by the Germans on April 9, 1940, and they had continued their fight from there. They were unwilling to capitulate to the Germans. Crown Prince Olav, who later became King Olav V, had extensive military training and was appointed to the post of Norwegian head of defense. Together, with some representatives from the Norwegian government, he returned to Norway on May 12, 1945.

If you hear a story enough times, you may come to think it is a part of your memory. For that reason, I am not 100 percent sure that I remember what happened on June 7, 1945; maybe I think I remember it because my father told me the story so many times. In a way, it is not so important. June 7, 1945, was the day when the rest of the royal family, including the king, Haakon VII, and the rest of the government returned to Oslo. While the king, the crown prince, and the government had been in exile in London, the crown princess and their three children had been in exile in the United States of America. They now arrived in Oslo together. What I think I remember is the following: My father took me in my stroller to see the royal family and the government returning to a free Norway. It was a sunny day, and we passed the park where the royal castle is. He pointed that out to me and told me that the king would certainly have a uniform on. Every time I saw a person with a uniform, whether it was a conductor on one of the streetcars, a police officer, or a military person, I asked my father, "Is that the king?" We continued down to the harbor, where the king arrived onboard the British Royal Navy ship *HMS Norfolk*. The harbor was packed with people; everybody cheered, sang "God Save the King" and the Norwegian national anthem, and waved the Norwegian flag. My father had given me a flag too, which I remember waving all the time.

Gradually life got back to normal both for adults and for children, and I could play outside the apartment and make friends.

My first friend was a boy named Arne. His grandmother owned one of the boarding houses, and he and his parents lived there until around 1946, when they moved to an apartment in another part of the city. He was six months older than I was, and we played together every day when he lived by his grandmother. After they moved, he visited his grandmother every weekend, and we continued to be great friends for a number of years—until we were around nine, when it was not so much fun for boys and girls to play together anymore.

My first girlfriend was Solveig. She lived across the street, so for a while our respective mothers had to help us crossing the street. From we were both around five, we were allowed to cross the street to each other on our own.

My paternal grandmother had gone with my father and his siblings on vacation every summer to the southern part of Norway where she was born. During the War, however, it was both difficult and risky to travel. Once the War was over, we went—my grandmother, my Aunts Kilda and

Marie, my mother, my father, and I. We left Oslo on June 22, 1945, on board *S/S Kristiansand*, which was a steamship going nonstop to Risør, where we would get off before continuing to the city of Arendal and the city of Kristiansand. We left Oslo around ten o'clock at night and arrived in Risoer around six o'clock the next morning. I do not remember much from this first trip, but almost every summer until I was eighteen, we went either to the city of Risør itself or to the small village of Fie, which was outside Risør.

Risør had around three thousand inhabitants in 1945 and has around forty-five hundred today. It is an old city. It is still called the White City by the Skagerak, since all the houses are painted white. (Skagerak is a strait running between the southeast coast of Norway, the southwest coast of Sweden, and the Jutland peninsula of Denmark, connecting the North Sea and the Kattegat Sea area, which leads to the Baltic Sea.) The number of inhabitants in the city of Risør itself and in its surroundings increased a lot during the summer, since many people came from Oslo to spend time in their summerhouses or with family like us.

After arriving in Risør in the early morning, we were picked up by one of my grandmother's brothers, Uncle Karsten, in his open fishing boat. The boat was around twenty-five feet, and it must have been packed with all of our luggage and us. My mother told me that the first time he picked us up, she was scared, but I guess after a few years she got used to it. I enjoyed the trip every summer, even when the weather was not perfect. As I have mentioned earlier, memory is interesting. During all my summer vacations as a child, I cannot remember it raining often; if it rained, it was mostly at night. I do remember, however, one summer when the weather was not nice when we arrived—blustery, with a lot of rain. For that reason, they had decided to send a partly enclosed taxi boat instead of one of the open boats. I must have been around three years old and remember it well, since that was the only time I got seasick. I preferred the open fishing boat.

We were going to the small village of Fie, a little bit south of Risør. As I've said previously, Fie and the neighboring villages had (and maybe still have) a few hundred inhabitants each and a larger number during the summer. We were going to stay with Uncle Karsten and his wife, Aunt Olga. Uncle Karsten had, over a number of years, bought not only the property where their house was built but also a lot of surrounding land, mostly from his father-in-law. He was a fisherman, but he and his wife (as was the case with many others in the village) also farmed. In addition to the main house, they had a cow barn, a hay barn, a pigsty, and a henhouse. Next to the barn was the outhouse, which was nice and clean and never smelled bad. There were old magazines there, so you could read while using the outhouse. One magazine I really enjoyed reading was called *URD*, a women's magazine with a Christian profile. It had many more articles about art and culture than other women's magazines. Sometimes I was sitting there for so long reading that other family members had to knock on the door so they could use the outhouse!

The property also had a well with nice cold water. Before the house had a fridge, which was many years later, the fresh milk was kept in an aluminum bucket in the well.

The property had four big sweet cherry trees, two with red cherries and one with yellow cherries. When I got older, I used to climb the trees and pick cherries. From what I remember, the produce grown on the property consisted of strawberries, cabbage, carrots, and potatoes. There were also wild blackberries nearby.

The house had two floors and a basement. A part of the basement was for laundry. It also had a wood-burning brick oven where Aunt Olga made the most delicious bread I have ever tasted.

On the first floor was a kitchen (even though Aunt Olga would often cook in the basement) and two living rooms, one with a couch since the house was always open for people to stay for a short or long period, and a third room where Aunt Olga had her sewing machine and a couch. After Uncle Karsten died in 1947, she would also sleep in this room when we were visiting on summer vacation. Each side of the second floor had an alcove with a built-in bed. I would normally sleep in one of these rooms, both of which were cozy. In the first big bedroom Aunt Olga had her loom, where she made rag rugs.

There is a long tradition of making rag rugs in Norway. One uses old clothes, bed linens, curtains etc. All the various cloths are washed until no more color will run from them, ironed, and cut into long, thin pieces that are rolled into cloth balls and then used for weaving. My grandmother would always bring old clothes for Aunt Olga to use. Before the clothes were washed and cut, my second cousins and I were allowed to dress up in them, which we loved. This room also had a canopy bed. When we played hide-and-seek, this was a great place to hide.

There was also another big bedroom, which was where my mother and father would normally sleep when we visited.

For a city girl, spending three weeks every summer at this house was paradise. Most of my father's cousins had children around my age whom I could play with. We could roam around without being afraid of traffic, as there were very few cars around. The only thing we had to learn early was to swim, which I did. I learned to fish using mussels or snails as bait that I crushed with a stone, and I eventually learned to clean the fish I caught.

Several days a week we had to go to the general store to shop and to check for mail. All the mail was called out by name, one at a time. We normally had the daily newspaper we subscribed to in Oslo delivered to us.

After three wonderful weeks, which always went too fast, we would return to Oslo.

While my mother cleaned the offices in a publisher's house three nights a week, I would spend time with my father, who would tell stories or read to me. He also started to teach me simple math and the alphabet. When I was four years old, I could count to twenty and add and subtract numbers between one and ten, and when I was five I could read. That opened up new worlds for me.

Until I was in my early teens, I was often sick. In addition to the normal childhood diseases, I got polio when I was around three years old. Luckily, it did not have any permanent negative impact on me, but I do remember that I suddenly could not walk for a while and that my mother cried. My parents managed to nurse me back to health, as they always did, and everybody, in particular my grandmothers, gave me all the nutritious food they could think of. Every winter I would get the bronchitis I mentioned earlier. I was also skinny and growing fast. When I was around five years old, our doctor recommended that I be sent to a sanatorium for children with asthma or bronchitis outside Oslo for six weeks to improve my health. The sanatorium had been established around the time the War ended and was run by Oslo Red Cross. While six weeks was a long time to be away from one's parents at that age, I survived. I was, of course, elated to return back home.

Just after I turned five, my baby brother was born. He was named

Hans Thomas after our maternal and paternal grandfathers (and also after our father Thomas). Hans was a beautiful baby—he had curly chestnut hair, and everybody talked about how wonderful he looked. Having had everybody's attention for the first five years of my life, I was jealous, at least for a little while. But I soon realized it was nice to have a brother, and I liked to be Big Sister. When he got bigger, I enjoyed dressing him up in girls' clothes, which he, of course, hated. Once, when I went to the bathroom while babysitting him, he managed to run out with the girls' clothes on—and I had to race after him to catch him. I was furious and hit him.

Two elderly ladies stopped and said, "Do not hit those who are smaller than you."

I looked at them and said, "But he is my brother," as if that legitimized my hitting him.

Most of the time we played together. He reluctantly agreed to play with my paper dolls if I would later play with his cars or use the metal construction set, which came with many perforated pieces and screws we could use to construct cranes, towers, and many other things. (This was many years before Lego came to Norway.) I would not admit it to Hans, but I actually enjoyed creating things with the construction toys.

A new chapter in my life was soon approaching—I was going to start school, and I was looking forward to it very much.

3

Growing Up

In early 1950, I went with my mother to enroll in the closest primary school. Classes would start in the middle of August.

The education system in Norway was different when I went to school from what it is today. It has actually changed a few times since I finished school, including the age at which one starts primary school and the length of mandatory education.

When I went to school, students started primary school the year they were seven years old. That meant that children, like myself, who were born in December, would start when they were six and a half years old. Mandatory education was seven years of primary school, and you could start working when you were fourteen years old.

I still remember the first day of school. I wore a sailor outfit, which was very popular at the time. It consisted of a marine pleated skirt and a red top with a navy sailor collar and white stripes. My mother had also braided a part of my hair on the top with red, white, and blue silk ribbons, the colors of the Norwegian flag. I had a small red knapsack in which I kept a wooden pencil case with a crayon that was red on one end (for writing the vowels) and blue on the other end (for writing the consonants). We were thirty girls, assembled with our mothers in the classroom. While all primary schools in Oslo were coed, girls and boys were in separate classes, and even the schoolyard was divided. There was no fence dividing us, but one part of the schoolyard was for girls and the other part for boys. The teacher was young; I am not quite sure, but I think it was her first teaching assignment. She called us one at a time by name and showed us which desk to occupy.

I soon made a best friend, Inger-Johanne. We had two things in common: we were both born in December, which made us the youngest in the class, and we both had younger brothers. While I was tall for my age, she was short, and the difference also attracted us to each other. While it made the walk to school longer for me, most days I would leave home a little early so I could stop by Inger-Johanne's and we could walk together to school. The walk would take me around thirty minutes. We also often played together in the afternoon after our homework.

Before we started school in the morning, we had to attend a thirty-minute school breakfast called "The Oslo Meal," which had been started in some Oslo schools in the mid-1930s to improve nutrition, particularly among children from working-class families. It would become important for those of us who had been born during the War. This initiative gained attention and was replicated in other countries, including Australia and the United States. The Oslo Meal normally consisted of two slices of bread with cheese, a cup of milk, and a carrot. To make sure that we got enough vitamins, they brushed one side of the bread with cod liver oil, which I really did not like.

Around the time I started school, my parents also started to send me to Sunday school. I had been to Sunday school from time to time in the churches my grandmothers belonged to, but I was baptized and belonged to what until recently was the Church of Norway, a Lutheran Protestant church. My parents felt it was important that I went to Sunday school in our parish church. Our parish church had just been restored and changed names from Our Saviour's Church to Oslo Cathedral in 1950, in connection with Oslo's celebration of its nine-hundredth anniversary. The church had a parish house on our street, so it was easy for me to attend Sunday school and walk to the parish house by myself. The parish house had two parish nurses who also ran the Sunday school from nine to ten o'clock every Sunday morning, apart from school holidays. Every child who attended had a card with his or her name on it, and a star was stamped on the card for every attendance. For every tenth attendance, we got a gold star. I liked Sunday school and enjoyed hearing stories both from the Old Testament and the New Testament. It was there I first heard about

Africa and, in particular, about Madagascar, where there were a number of Norwegian missionaries. I liked Sunday school and liked to ask questions. My paternal grandmother and my aunt Kilda gave me a Children's Bible for Christmas after I started school. It had pictures in color and in black and white, and while it had around six hundred pages, it was written in a way that was easier to understand for children.

School was disappointing for the first couple of years. I did not really learn much, so I found it boring. During the winter months, I continued often to be ill with colds and bronchitis and could not go to school. The teacher brought homework to our home on a regular basis (which I doubt they do today), and I always finished it fast. I somewhat enjoyed staying home, since it meant I could read other books, and my parents, who worked in a printing office and a publisher's house, always managed to find a number of good books for me to read. From I was around nine years old, they also allowed med to read books that were not especially for children, which I found even more exciting. I remember in particular some books in the series called *Our Own Saga*: it was ten books by different Norwegian authors that focused on the Norwegian resistance and underground forces during the Second World War.

In 1951, the first volume of a new encyclopedia was published. I cannot recall whether it was my mother or father who brought it home, since my mother's company published it and my father's company printed it. It ultimately consisted of four volumes: the next two volumes came out in 1952, and the last one in 1953. It was called *Skattkista* in Norwegian, which means "the treasure chest," an apt name. It consisted of short encyclopedic articles in alphabetical order and a selection of longer articles that went more in depth on certain issues. I read the books from cover to cover as soon as we got them, and they opened many new worlds for me. I still have the books on my bookshelf.

Just after I started school, I also joined the Girl Scouts, where I acquired a number of new skills. We went camping, which I had never done before—and have not done since! Their focus on being prepared has, however, followed me for my entire life.

When I started fourth grade, everything changed. I started to love school and found it suddenly both interesting and challenging. To my teacher's big surprise, I suddenly became the best student in mathematics class. During these years, at least in some schools, there were different mathematics curriculums for girls and boys; the one for boys was more demanding. The fact that I continued to be ill during a part of the winter suddenly became an advantage. I finished all the mathematics tests and homework at home, so the teacher decided to give me the math books for boys as well, which I excelled at. If I had not been ill, I would not have discovered the different math books. That gave me something to think about.

Most people living on the west side of Oslo were relatively well off. Most of the girls in my class had fathers who were doctors, lawyers, or business owners. Most mothers stayed at home, but I remember one mother was a teacher and another one a medical doctor. I was invited to some of the girls' homes, sometimes for birthday parties. They all lived in big apartments and had maids and nannies if they had smaller siblings. I knew my parents were intelligent people; had they been given the opportunity for more education, they would easily have been able to compete with many of my schoolmates' parents. Like so many others from working-class families, they both had to start working at the age of fourteen, as soon as they finished primary school. I realized at a relatively young age that it would be important for me to get more education than my parents if I were to be able to compete for a good job and move up in society.

While the demand for affordable housing in Oslo had constantly increased during the last few years before the War and had increased a lot during the War, it increased even more just after the War ended. No new apartments had been built during the War, and the local government authorities in Oslo had to find ways to increase new apartment construction. One way to rent an affordable apartment was to get on a waiting list at the Oslo Municipal Apartment Building Office, which was what my father did shortly after the War ended. I remember a few years later, around the time I started school, that my father said that there were around fifteen thousand families on the waiting list.

There were some who criticized the government for being too slow in building apartments. One who was very vocal was an engineer called Olav Selvaag. He wrote an open letter to the Norwegian parliament and sent copies to leading newspapers; in it he criticized residential regulations and codes for their inefficiency and claimed that many more residences could be built with the same amount of materials and effort. His persistent philosophy was that our society owed it to itself to use all its available resources to benefit as many citizens as possible—especially those who were disadvantaged. After a few years, the government decided to allocate 350 acres of land to Selvaag and his company around ten miles northeast of the city center, a place called Veitvet. The first apartment buildings were two-and four-family townhouses and were finished in 1953.

That year, my parents learned that they would be allocated an apartment at Veitvet in the next building phase. These apartments would be different from those in the first phase. Using a unconventional approach, Selvaag decided to build duplex apartments with internal staircases. The building where we were allocated an apartment had thirty-two three-bedroom duplex apartments and sixteen one-bedroom apartments. The three-bedroom apartments were on floors one through four, and the small apartments were on the ground floor at the back of the building. Access to the apartments on the third and fourth floors was through staircases on each side of the building; these led up to a long balcony on the front of the building, where all the entrances to the apartments were. We were allocated an apartment on the third and fourth floors of the building. The apartment complexes were organized as co-ops. Each owner of the large apartments had to pay five thousand Norwegian kroner (approximately nine hundred dollars, using the present exchange rate) to get a share in the co-op; the rest was financed by low-interest-rate loans through the Norwegian State Housing Bank, a state-owned bank that had been established in 1946 to assist in financing the building of apartments and houses after the War. I do not know what my parents' salaries were at the time, but I knew from discussions they had that five thousand kroner was a lot of money for them. One way or another, they managed to raise the necessary funds. One always hears about buildings costing more than anticipated by the time they are finished. In this case, it was different. The final costs were lower than first anticipated, and the payment for the individual shares was reduced to 4,700 kroner.

We were told that we could to move in around August or September 1954, so that summer my parents decided that we would not go on our usual summer vacation to Risør. They decided instead that I would go for six weeks to a summer camp run by the City of Oslo; the camp was a couple of hours southwest of the city. I had already attended summer camp for three weeks the year before at a camp run by our parish church, and I really liked that. The camp I attended had only girls, but there was a similar camp for boys in the same area.

I cannot remember exactly how many girls we were, but I think we were around fifty. We had our meals in a large dining hall on the first floor, where there was also a large kitchen. On the second floor were three dormitories for the girls and bedrooms for the staff members. Latrines were in a separate building. There was also another building with a partly open common shower facility. There were activities every day—we went to the beach, went on hiking trips, had various sport competitions, and more. If it rained heavily, we would have activities inside. Parents and other relatives had been informed in advance that they could send packages with chocolate and other sweets, biscuits, and similar things, but the content of all packages would be combined and shared every Saturday. This made a lot of sense, since not everybody got packages from home. My parents sent something every week, along with letters that I responded to. I enjoyed the summer camp, but not everybody did. There were even some girls who tried to run away. One of the girls at the summer camp, Berit, went to the school I would be enrolled in after we moved; she was at the same grade level, fifth grade, and suggested that I should try to get in the same class as her. I thought this would be great, as I at least would know one person at the new school.

We moved as planned in early September 1954. Hans and I spent the day of the move with my aunt Marit and her husband Harald, and we also spent the night there. When we arrived in the new apartment the next afternoon, most things were already in place. The apartment was around one thousand quare feet, but for us it was enormous. On the first floor of the apartment was a hallway with a small wood-burning oven, which could be used to heat the apartment in addition to electric radiators. That floor also had a large eat-in kitchen. What was remarkable at that time was the fact that each of these apartments came with a small built-in refrigerator. That would make things so much easier, as we wouldn't have to worry about the milk or other things going bad, and we would not need to shop every day during the summer since we now had a cold place to store food. The bathroom was also on this floor. It came with a bathtub and shower and had hot and cold water available from the tap—something we had never had before. On the second floor were the living room and two additional bedrooms—one for me and one for my brother Hans. This was absolutely fantastic. Hans and I found the place so big, with so many rooms. It was perfect for playing hide-and-seek.

The next day I went with my mother to register at the new school. My old school had sent all the necessary papers to this new school, so they already had me in their system. To get to the school, we had to take the bus. While the school was not that far away, there were actually six bus stops between Veitvet, where we now lived, and Grorud, which was a little bit further north and where I was going to attend school. There was one school a little bit closer, but they did not yet admit students at my grade level. By the time the neighborhood school was built at Veitvet, I had finished primary school. Since there were many children who had moved to Veitvet who were at my grade level, the school decided to establish a coed class for these children. All the other classes were for just girls or just boys. However, since I had asked to be placed in the same class as Berit, who I had met at the summer camp, the school principal agreed to put me in that class instead of the class with the other children from Veitvet. There were a few girls who had lived in the area before and who had moved to Veitvet in my class as well. I made a number of friends: Kari, Liv, Targjerd, and Mette, to mention a few.

I know Kari has passed away, and many years had passed since I saw the others—when one day, something exciting happened. I got a friend request from Mette on Facebook. I remembered Mette well for many reasons. She lived at Veitvet as well and had gone to the Grorud primary school since first grade. She was as short as I was tall for my age, and she had problems at school. I tried to help her with homework and other things. When we reconnected through Facebook, she told me that many years later it was discovered that she was dyslexic. When we were young, no tests were performed to understand the kinds of challenges students might have. Unfortunately, students in that category were often considered to be slow learners. She said that it was thanks to me that she passed her final exams in math, and she certainly still remembered it and was grateful for all my help. When I visited Oslo a few years ago, Mette and I had lunch together. We had then not seen each other in fifty-five years. It was wonderful to reconnect, and we had so much to talk about. We continue to be in regular contact.

For the first time I had a male teacher as for homeroom at my new school. His name was Alfred Buer, and he had been a missionary in Africa. He was a kind man and made me feel welcome immediately. We had him as a teacher in most subjects.

I did well at school. While I had earned top grades in math in my previous school, I now also got top grades in most other subjects at my new school. The only subjects in which I did not receive top grades were physical education, art, handwriting, and the like.

Our homeroom teacher was unfortunately often sick. He had contracted malaria while in Africa, and when the school year ended in June 1955, he had to leave on disability pension and died later that year.

In addition to my homeroom teacher, the school's principal was also a man, and he taught us geography. The only women teachers I had this first year were for physical education and handicraft. In handicraft we learned needlework, knitting, and sewing. One of our projects was to make the uniforms we were to use in physical education classes. When I started sixth grade, in August 1955, we got a new homeroom teacher, Signe Fjalestad. She was an experienced teacher, but also strict. I did not know it then, but she would have a major impact on my continuing education and life.

Two new subjects were added to the curriculum, home economics and English. Today children start with English at school much earlier, often in the first grade, and they are also exposed to English in so many extracurricular ways, particularly through television.

I liked home economics, where we learned to cook a number of dishes. We also learned how to shop for some of the ingredients, and through that, we got a better idea of the cost of food.

I also loved learning English and got top grades in it from the start. I knew it would open new worlds for me since it would enable me to read books in English. In the beginning, I went to the library to borrow relatively uncomplicated books in English. It took me much longer to read them than the Norwegian books, but after a while I got the hang of it. Our English teacher was good, but she had most likely not spent much time in an English-speaking country. This was not strange, since only ten years had passed since World War II had ended, so the opportunities to travel abroad were still somewhat limited. While we learned correct English grammar, expressions, and spelling, we all spoke with a heavy Norwegian accent, which I still have not been able to get rid of entirely.

One day I read about an international pen-pal club in a Norwegian magazine. The club was called Youth of All Nations. I contacted them, and they sent me a form to fill out with details about myself, including age, interests, and what languages I could read and write. That was the start of my getting a number of pen pals from different countries. I had pen pals from Denmark, Finland, New Zealand, the United States, and India. Apart from the pen pals from Denmark and Finland, with whom I could communicate in Norwegian, the others were in English. While it took time to write in English in the beginning, this also assisted me in improving my English further. Having never been outside of Norway, it also taught me about other countries and cultures over and above what I learned in my geography and history lessons at school.

I exchanged letters with some of my pen pals for short periods, some much longer. A few years later, when I was around eighteen, I had one pen pal left, Sarah from India. We continued to exchange letters for a few more years, but around the time we were both twenty-one, we lost touch. I knew that Sarah had moved to London to study law. I had also moved a couple of times and had gotten married, and we lost each other's addresses. From time to time, I thought about Sarah and how nice it would be to be in touch again, but I did not know how. More than thirty years later, still thinking about her from time to time, I got an idea—I used modern technology and searched online for her name. I did not get any results, but I got a person called David with the same surname living in Washington, DC. I also managed to find David's email address. I thought I remembered that Sarah had a brother called David, but I was not sure it was the right person. Still, I decided to send David an email, explaining who I was and why I was contacting him.

The answer came back fast, saying roughly, "Sarah is certainly my sister; she is living in London; this is her phone number, email address, and regular address; and I have already called her and told her about you contacting me."

Sarah and I had never heard each other's voices. We had seen pictures of each other when we were much younger, but we had never seen each other in person. I looked at the time, took into account the time difference, and then called. It was exciting and emotional for both of us. Sarah had also been thinking about me. She even remembered when my birthday was. A few months later, Sarah told me she would be transiting through New York for one day after a Christmas visit to see her father and brother in Washington DC. The day was New Year's Day. I invited her for brunch at Ambassador Grill on Forty-Fourth Street in Manhattan, and there we saw each other in person for the first time. It was fantastic; we talked for hours over champagne and good food and later went to my office, which was just across the street. While we have not seen each other since that day, we continue to be in touch on a regular basis.

As I have already mentioned, when I was going to school, only seven years of primary school were mandatory. There were many options after that, from starting work to one year of secondary education and then starting an apprenticeship program or, on the other end of the scale, to enrolling in five years of secondary education, which would result in a high school diploma and entitle one to enroll in a university.

While my parents fully agreed that I should have some secondary education, they, and particularly my mother, felt that I should start working as soon as possible. Their idea was that I should take one year of secondary education and then some typing and bookkeeping classes that could prepare me to get a job in an office. I had to inform my homeroom teacher about this plan, since the necessary forms for enrollment in any secondary school had to go through her and the principal. After a day or two, she asked to see me. She said she had been thinking a lot about what I told her. While any secondary education was free, one had to pay for books and other things, and she fully understood that that was not easy for my parents. But she also strongly felt that because I was such a promising student, further education would give me so many additional opportunities and open up so many additional doors. For that reason, she would be willing to assist me financially through a loan that I would only have to pay back when I started to work. She said she would be willing to give me enough to cover books and other things I needed for school, including necessary clothes. She would expect me to work during parts of the summer vacation to earn additional money. She wanted to meet with my parents to discuss this plan. After having told them about this that night, my parents discussed it among themselves. The following day they told me that they thought this was a great plan and that my father wanted to meet with my homeroom teacher at her convenience. Everything was agreed upon, and I enrolled in secondary school.

After I graduated from primary school, my father arranged for me to work as a messenger in his printing house for a few weeks until our summer vacation. Since I was not yet fourteen, I was only allowed to work thirty-six hours a week, compared to the forty-eight hours that comprised the regular work week at that time. Everybody worked on Saturdays as well, but only until one o'clock in the afternoon. I enjoyed the work. I delivered letters and samples of special print, collected checks to be deposited at the bank, and felt like an adult with a lot of responsibility. While I knew the city of Oslo well, I became even more familiar with all the streets around the center of the city. I was paid on a weekly basis and was proud when I got my first salary. I was allowed to spend some of the money on clothes; I remember buying my first pair of Wrangler blue jeans, which had just come on the market in Oslo.

The summer went fast, and in the middle of August I started secondary school. For the first time, I was in a coed class, which was exciting. In addition to our homeroom teacher, we had many other teachers. An additional foreign language, German, was also added to our curriculum. The German teacher was great both as a teacher and as a human being. While I did well in German, I was not enticed to read a lot of German books. I remember, however, that in addition to what was mandatory reading at school, I went to the library and borrowed Erich Maria Remarque's book, *Im Western nichts Neues* (*All Quiet on the Western Front*), which is about the stress of soldiers during World War I. I continued to get a number of books in English from the library—I remember borrowing novels, such as *1984* and *Brave New World*. My parents continued to get books from their respective jobs, and I read through all the volumes of *The Forsyte Saga* by John Galsworthy in Norwegian translation. That would come in handy a few years later when I would study a part of it in English literature. Since I had read it in Norwegian, I knew the stories well.

In January 1958, I started classes once a week at night in preparation for my June confirmation at church. The pastor was a likable and colorful person. The parish church at Veitvet was not finished yet, so we would be confirmed at Grorud Church, which was just across the street from where I had attended primary school.

I am a great believer that things happen for a reason and that you meet people for a reason. While I still had a year or so to decide, decisions would have to be made about which area to specialize in after the first two years of secondary school. The last three years, which would lead to a high school diploma at that time, would normally give you the option to specialize in math and science or in languages. I was good at both— maybe slightly better in math and science—so the choice would not be easy.

Then I met Grethe, who was attending the same confirmation preparation as I was. She was one year older than most of us and had for some reason waited a year to be confirmed. She would finish the two years of secondary school just after confirmation and start the last three years that fall, so she had already had to make her choice. I discovered then that there was a third alternative that I was not aware of. It was only offered in one school in the greater Oslo area, and its focus was on business administration, economics, and law, in addition to the regular subjects of math and languages. She told me that one had to have excellent grades to be admitted, since space was limited. Some students took a third year of secondary school to get extra credits to be admitted. The school, which is called Oslo Handelsgymnasium (Oslo Commercial High School), was on the west side of Oslo, not far from where we'd lived before moving to Veitvet. That meant a relatively long bus ride every morning and afternoon.

I had already made up my mind: this school had a perfect curriculum for me. I would get my high school diploma, but it would include subjects that would assist me in getting a good job just after high school. My parents thought it was a good idea, so I now had a further incentive to work hard at school to get top grades.

Since I now had turned fourteen, I could work full-time during part of the summer vacation, and I managed to get a job in one of the grocery stores owned by Oslo Cooperative Society. I was helping in the meat section, packing cheese, delivering groceries to people living in the neighborhood, and many other things. One of our customers was the Norwegian prime minister at that time, Einar Gerhardsen, and his wife, Werna. There was no prime minister's residence at that time, nor was there any special security for him. That has since changed. Einar Gerhardsen represented the Labor Party and first became prime minister in 1945, just after World War II ended. He was prime minister during three periods, all together for seventeen years, making him the longest serving prime minister in Norway so far. I spoke often to Werna Gerhardsen when she visited the store, and she often asked me to carry groceries for her to their apartment. I saw Prime Minister Gerhardsen a few times, but my conversations with him were limited to "Good afternoon" or "Hello."

I applied to Oslo Commercial High School the following year and was admitted without any problems.

In the late spring, my mother told me some even more exciting news: she was unexpectedly pregnant again. She was forty-three years old and had not planned to have another child. While abortion was not generally legalized yet in Norway, she was given the option because of her age. She decided not to. I was excited to have another sister or brother. The baby would be born around my sixteenth birthday so he or she would in many ways almost get two mothers. My parents asked me not to take a summer job that summer and to instead be at home to help my mother and to go with my father and Hans to Risør for summer vacation. My mother would join us one week into our vacation.

My mother had changed jobs the previous November. A big shopping center had been built at Veitvet; it was the largest in northern Europe at that time and the first real shopping center in Norway. One of the shops that was to open was divided in two: it would sell newspapers, magazine, sweets, and cigarettes in the front part, and it would sell ice cream, hot dogs, and sodas in the other part. That is where my mother started to work. She enjoyed this very much and was well liked by everybody, particularly many of the young people who came to buy ice cream or hot dogs.

I was excited when school started in August. Every morning I had to take a bus just after seven o'clock in the morning to reach school by eight, but I did not mind. There were many new subjects. In Norwegian, English, and German, we learned how to write business letters and had other business-related subjects in addition to literature and essays. When I started the second year at school, French was also added. We also had accounting, business administration, law, economics, and more traditional subjects, such as math, history, and geography, but even these subjects were related to business in the curriculum. History, for example, had a lot on the industrial revolution. Typewriting was also mandatory, both for boys and girls. I still, however, remember what our English teacher told us girls: "When you start working, do not tell anybody that you can type. If you do, they will automatically use you as their secretary, even if you were hired to do something else."

There were twelve boys and twelve girls in my class, but there were more boys than girls in our high school. We had around 175 students at my grade level, 75 girls and 100 boys; more than 400 prospective students had applied. My homeroom teacher was also my business administration teacher, and but we had different teachers in all the other subjects. The school had for many years been able to attract excellent teachers in all the subjects being taught, which we benefitted from. The code of conduct for teachers and students was high. The teachers did not use first names when addressing students; the girls were "Miss So-and-So" and the boys were addressed using only their last names. Girls had to wear a dress or a skirt—the only days we were allowed to wear pants were Saturdays and days before holidays.

The transition period was difficult. Being used to getting top grades in most subjects, I was shocked when I got my report card after the first two months. I had lower grades in most subjects and even "less than satisfactory" in one subject. I had to do better! I started to work even more systematically, interacted more in discussions, and in many ways worked smarter and harder. And it paid off. By Christmas, when we got our midterm grades, I had improved in all subjects and again earned top grades in many of them.

The US opened its new embassy building in the summer of 1959. The building was around a five-minute walk from my school. The security was very different back then, and the entrance on the east side of the building gave the public access to the United States Information Service Library. I went there often to borrow books and also sometimes did my homework there.

The school had a fantastic great hall or *aula*, as it was called. It was used for many activities, including wonderful jazz concerts, debates, Christmas balls, and graduation ceremonies. The great hall also had an organ especially built for the great hall; it was like a church organ. We had one teacher who was also an organist. Once a week, during the noon recess, he would play on the organ, and we, the students and the other teachers, loved it. It was a big treat.

On December 18, 1959, I turned sixteen, and the following morning, December 19, my mother gave birth to another boy. This time she decided on the name, which was Morten. I loved my baby brother, and in many ways he indeed had two mothers. Over the next few years, I would babysit him as often as I had time and also would often take him with me when I went out. And despite the fact that he is very tall, 196 centimeters (6 feet 4 inches), I still consider him in many ways my baby brother.

Before the summer vacation started, I had to find a summer job. While Miss Fjalestad, whom I saw regularly, was pleased with my progress and had not set any upper limit for how much she was willing to lend me, I knew I had to pay it back when I finished school. So supplements from summer jobs were very important. Checking around, I found an interesting job at the headquarters of a company called Narvesen Kiosk Company. The company was well known and interesting. Bertrand Narvesen, a traveling mail clerk, had established it in 1894. He traveled by train from Christiania (which was Oslo's name at the time) to various places southwest of the capital. He realized fast that people needed something to read while traveling, so he applied to the state-owned railway company to be allowed to open newsstands at some of the stations. This was a success and was gradually expanded. By the time I joined, the company had newsstands or kiosks at all the railway stations throughout Norway and additional kiosks or small stores in the biggest cities. The people who ran the kiosks or newsstands had to send in the accounts four times a year to be audited by headquarters. My job was to do the audit. What was great for me was that they wanted me to come work not only during the summer but during any vacation I had from school. I continued to work for Narvesen during all my vacations, until I finished school, and I took only two weeks off during the summer. I found the job interesting and liked the people I worked with. From time to time, I also substituted at the switchboard.

The three years at Oslo Handelsgymnasium went fast. The final exams were to take place in May and early June 1962: seven days of written exams in seven different subjects and one oral exam on a subject that was decided randomly from five different options by drawing.

But then in April, I got sick. I first thought it was an ordinary stomach bug, but I got a very high fever, so my mother called the doctor. At that time doctors still did house calls, so the doctor came to examine me, and he was concerned. What had maybe started as a stomach bug had developed into a serious infection and then to pneumonia. He decided I had to be hospitalized. I was devastated. I had to be well in time for the exams. I stayed at the hospital for two weeks, where they gave me all kinds of medications. I tried to study as much as possible in preparation for the exams, but I was weak and got easily tired. I was, however, thrilled when I was allowed to go home. I was feeling much better but was told to take it easy and not participate in many of the pre-graduation festivities.

The time for exams finally started, and I tried to do my best. When the results were published, I was reasonably pleased, everything taken into account. I did not get the top grade in French or law. However, I got a top grade in English, which was slightly better than expected. In all the other subjects I did as well as expected.

On June 23, 1962, a midsummer day in Norway, I was the first in my entire family to graduate from high school. The ceremony took place in the school's great hall, and we all marched in to the tune of "Pomp and Circumstance" on the organ. The girls wore white dresses or suits, and the boys wore suits, and all of us had our black student caps on. My father was there to witness it all. He had taken the day off from work, which by itself was unusual. I was elated he was there, and I know he was proud of me.

I had finished an important part of my life, and the future lay ahead of me.

4

Marriage, Motherhood, and Much More

After a well deserved two-week vacation in Risør, it was time to get a job. Narvesen Kiosk Company, where I had worked every vacation during the last three years, was more than willing to hire me. However, I was looking for something different, with more challenges. The salary was also important. While Miss Fjalestad was pleased with what I had achieved so far and was not rushing me in starting to pay back the money I owed her, I wanted to start paying back the five thousand Norwegian kroner (around nine hundred dollars) as soon as possible.

I saw an advertisement in the paper announcing that one of the nation's largest commercial banks, Christiania Bank, had several open entry-level positions. I decided to give them a call. We did not have a phone at home, so I had to go to the nearest telephone booth to call the human resources department. The lady I talked to sounded nice, and she asked me to bring my high school diploma and all other relevant papers from my vacation jobs for an interview two days later, which I did.

Christiania Bank was not only one of the largest commercial banks but also the oldest commercial bank in Norway, established in 1848. Its headquarters was near one of the main squares in Oslo, Stortorvet (meaning "the grand plaza"). A fire in 1624 destroyed much of the medieval city of Oslo, and when the city was rebuilt it was moved westward to be closer to the Akershus Fortress, which is at the mouth of the Oslofjord. The king, Christian IV of Denmark/Norway, then renamed the city Christiania after himself, and a number of companies, including Christiania Bank, used the name as a part of their company name. (The city's name was changed back to Oslo in 1924, three hundred years after the name change.)

Christiania Bank had a number of branches throughout Oslo in 1962. It had also acquired some smaller banks outside Oslo; these became a part of Christiania Bank and were under the guidance of the headquarters in Oslo, but they had a separate board of directors.

The lady with whom I had talked on the phone conducted my interview. After a while, she asked me to wait in her office, and she took my paper and her notes to another office, which turned out to belong to the director of human resources. I cannot remember how long I had to wait; it felt like eternity. I was then asked to see the director himself, Mr. Rasmussen, a middle-aged man with a serious look. He looked down at the papers, said that he was impressed with my education and work experience, and that the bank would be happy to hire me on a one-year temporary contract. If they were satisfied with my work, I would be offered a permanent contract after one year. He offered me a job as a bank assistant in one of the branches; I'd be serving the customers of the branch. The salary for the first year would be one thousand Norwegian kroner a month (approximately $150), and after one year the salary would increase. (I discovered fairly fast that all the banks had two salary scales, one for women and one for men; this changed late in 1962, and I benefitted by getting a small raise even before one year had passed.) I planned a careful budget in which I would try to put into a saving account one hundred kroner a month, pay miss Fjalestad two hundred kroner a month, and pay my parents two hundred kroner a month. For the first two months, I would be placed in a branch that was used for training new recruits. During the training period, I would be continually evaluated, and when the trainers felt I was ready, I would be placed at another branch. Mr. Rasmussen wanted me to start the following week. The branch used for training was only two bus stops from where I lived in Veitvet, which was perfect.

Just before I left his office, Mr. Rasmussen looked up for the first time during our conversation and stated, "Miss Holmgrunn, please be aware that the bank expects you to style you hair in a decent way."

I was shocked and did not know what to say, but it did not seem that he expected an answer. I did not see anything indecent with my hairstyle. I had long, straight hair, neatly pinned on one side with a gold-colored pin. I had no plans to change my hairstyle in response of his comment. A few years later, I did cut my hair much shorter, but only because my new perm did not look good on me. I never permed my hair again.

Interestingly, Mr. Rasmussen later came to visit the branch where I worked. When he saw me, he said, "Now your hair looks nice." Unbelievable!

The branch was relatively new. It had opened less than five years earlier in one of the new suburbs that, like Veitvet, had been built during the early-to-mid-1950s. The branch was located just at the outskirts of the residential area by the main road. A pharmacy and a post office were in the same building. I was the only trainee at the time, which was great since the staff could spend more time explaining everything. It was also July, which was the main vacation month in Norway and relatively quiet. Most of the customers were private customers, but there were also a number of neighborhood businesses. The private customers could, in addition to depositing or withdrawing money from their accounts, pay rent and utilities and apply for loans. Loans above a certain amount and business loans and credit lines had to be approved by headquarters. Private customers could also buy foreign exchange for vacation purposes, but there were still restrictions on how much they could buy, limited to three thousand kroner per year (about five hundred dollars).

This was before everything was computerized, and the bank had an elaborate system that was partly manual and partly used a huge accounting machine with one card for each customer's account. Every day, the interest on all interest-bearing accounts had to be entered manually, as did all transactions. I quickly learned the various systems and transaction types, and after one month the branch manager told me that he had recommended to headquarters that I was ready to be transferred to another branch. I had finished my trainee period.

The branch I was transferred to was in the northeastern past of Oslo, in an area called Torshov, which was not too far from the center of the city. It was notably different from the branch where I had had my training. The branch manager, who was in his mid-fifties, was a leader in the Boy Scouts movement and was also interested in local history, so on my first day he spent most of our time together giving me an overview of the Torshov area. He told me that the name meant "Thor's Temple," referring to the old Norse god, Thor—the god of thunder. The original temple was said to have been in the area, even though nothing had ever been found of it. It was believed, however, that the farm, which was also named Torshov and was built during the Middle Ages, was built on the ruins of the temple.

The customer base was a mix of big industrial companies, local stores, and private customers. The city had built a large number of apartments in the 1920s, and the bank was on the ground floor of one of these buildings and had been there since around 1930. One of the customers was Torshov School, which had been established in 1878 by Johan A. Lippestad as the first school in Norway for children with developmental and intellectual difficulties. The school had been built on the land where Torshov the farm had been, and it was later taken over by the state.

Among the customers was a famous soccer (or *football*, as most countries outside the United States refer to it) club named SKEID. They tended to be one of the top clubs in the Norwegian Football League. From time to time, they gave a bank branch a few tickets to games in Oslo, which we then raffled out among those who were interested to go. I loved football and went to several games with some of my colleagues. Almost all my colleagues were men. One of the women was Anna Maria, a Danish woman around five years older than I was. She had worked in banking in Denmark for a number of years but had decided to take a few years off to work in banking in Norway. We fast became close friends, and when I got married a year later, she was my maid of honor. Anna Maria went back to Denmark a few years later and continued to work in banking in Copenhagen until she retired. We have kept up over all of these years. We met in Copenhagen a few times when I went on business trips for one of the banks I worked at as well as when I visited UNICEF's supply division in Copenhagen. After she retired, she moved back to Tjaereborg in Jutland, Denmark, where she lives in the farmhouse where she grew up. While we have not seen each other since she moved, we still keep in touch and write long Christmas letters to each other.

A few months before I started to work, the first book club, the Norwegian Book Club, was launched in Norway. As I loved to read, I enrolled in the book club as soon as I started to work. Like most book clubs, they had a book-of-the-month that we would get automatically unless we declined the month before it was launched. The books were old as well as newer, and they were written in Norwegian or translated into it. The first three books were Sigrid Undset's *Kristin Lavransdatter*, a trilogy of historical novels called *The Wreath*, *The Wife*, and *The Cross*, published in 1920, 1921, and 1922, respectively. The books formed the basis of Sigrid Undset's receiving the 1928 Nobel Prize in Literature for her powerful description of life in Norway during the Middle Ages. I still have these three books and all the other books I bought through the book club over the years. I continued to be a member until I left Norway in 1985. I bought more than 250 books while I was a member.

During the last year of high school, students could be admitted to activities run by the Norwegian Student Association. From 1951, they had rented a place called Dovrehallen, on the east side of Oslo. Dovrehallen, named after the Hall of the Mountain King in the famous play, *Peer Gynt*, by Henrik Ibsen, had been a popular cabaret theater and tavern. It was originally established in 1900, and after being taken over by the Norwegian Student Association in 1951, it became a gathering place for informal gatherings, dances, musical entertainment, lecturers, and often-lively debates.

I liked the atmosphere in Dovrehallen, and after I started working, I went there from time to time on Saturdays. It was there that I met Knut. He was twenty-three years old, studied law, was active in many areas in the Norwegian Student Association, and was running a small tavern for the association in the basement of the building where the association had its offices. He was also working part-time as a telex operator for a shipping company.

We started to see each other often, sometimes in the tavern he was running, sometimes in Dovrehallen on Sundays, and occasionally in the office where he was a telex operator at night.

While I had had boyfriends before, this relationship started to be more serious; we fell in love, and everything was nice and rosy. I brought him home to meet my parents, and after some hesitation, he brought me home to meet his mother. He had already told me that his father was a chief engineer on board a Norwegian merchant ship that sailed internationally and that he was only home a few times a year. He had one brother, who was nine years younger than he was. His mother, who was originally from the city of Trondheim, worked at the Norwegian State Education Loan Fund, where she had been for many years. While his mother was cordial when we met, I sensed that she did not think I was good enough for her son. Knut later confirmed that but also said that I should not be concerned about it. He said she would warm up to me after a while, but he also mentioned in passing that she could be very difficult.

On my birthday in December, he asked me to marry him, and we got engaged. He wanted us to get married in the early-to-middle part of the following year, but he would have to consult with his father, who was coming home for Christmas, when he would return to Norway again in the spring or summer.

My parents were not too happy about my getting married. While women got married rather early during that period—the average age women got married for the first time was around twenty-one—they felt I was too young and should wait a while. I did not want to listen to that and managed to convince them that I was mature enough to get married and that I knew what I was doing.

I met Knut's father during Christmas. He was a nice man, quite different from Knut's mother. He had already informed Knut that he would return to Norway again in late June, so we planned the wedding date accordingly.

Knut knew a real-estate broker who helped us rent a fully furnished apartment close to the primary school I had attended at Grorud; our lease started in late June and lasted for around six months. The couple that owned it was going to Africa on a work assignment for those months. The friend told Knut that it would not be difficult to find another apartment to rent next.

Just before we got married, I got my permanent contract with Christiania Bank and a pay raise. I enjoyed my work and was looking forward to the future.

Knut had two unmarried aunts, sisters of his mother, living in Oslo; another unmarried aunt to whom he was very close, living in Trondheim; and his grandmother on his mother's side, who lived with her in their old family house. His grandfather had been a well-known businessman in Trondheim.

My parents could not afford to host a big wedding for us and suggested that we have a gathering at home for a limited number of people after the wedding ceremony. And so we did.

A few weeks after we got married, I went to the doctor, who confirmed what we had suspected for some time—I was pregnant. This was a time when no ultrasound existed, so the due date was calculated using the last time you had your period. I informed the doctor that I always had had an irregular period, but he did not seem to listen to that and indicated that the estimated due date would be January 10. Doing the calculation myself based on when I thought I would have become pregnant, I told the doctor that that most likely was one month too early, but again he did not listen to that.

Both Knut and I were thrilled about having a baby. We invited my parents for dinner and told them, and they were also happy about becoming grandparents, even though they had hoped we would have waited a few years. Knut sent a letter to his father, who had left Oslo by then, and decided to go to tell his mother alone. I do not know exactly what she said, but he told me that we could always say that the baby was premature when born, which I thought was very stupid.

The pregnancy went well. I was in good health, never sick at all, and in good shape. The paid maternity leave in Norway at that time was three months (today it is nine months with full pay or twelve months with three-quarter pay), plus any vacation time accumulated. I had decided to work until the end of the year, which would give me ten days until the estimated due date. I worked as much overtime as possible to earn extra money doing account closings before the year's end.

Just after Christmas we moved to a lovely single-family house on the west side of Oslo. We managed to afford the rent by taking over an existing tenant who rented one room and then renting out another room to another tenant.

The tenth of January came and went: no baby. By the twentieth, I went to the doctor for a checkup. Everything was fine, but he suggested that I should wait a few more days before getting admitted to the hospital. By twenty-fifth there was still no baby, and the doctor decided that I should be admitted to the hospital on January 29 to induce labor, which I did. After three hours in the hospital, I gave birth to a little baby girl who weighed six pounds, and the doctor at the hospital agreed with me that the due date most likely should have been February 10 instead of January 10.

After five days in the hospital, which was the norm at the time if a new mom had no complications, I went home with my little baby girl. She was so beautiful. Knut and I were so sure that the baby would be a girl that we had only decided on a girl's name: Elizabeth.

With the vacation time and what was left of my maternity leave, I would have to go back to work when Elizabeth was two and a half months old. I therefore immediately started making arrangements for who would take care of her while I was at work. My aunt Kilda had already mentioned that she and my grandmother knew a nice woman from church who took care of two children, so after a few weeks I took Elizabeth in the baby pram and visited Mrs. Skorpen—or Auntie Skorpen, as she was called by the children she took care of and their parents. She was absolutely the perfect person, warm and caring. She was taking care of two other children at that time and had no problems taking in another one. She also lived not too far from the branch of Christiania Bank where I would work after my maternity leave ended. We agreed on the pay and that I would bring Elizabeth to her every morning before going to work and pick her up after work. We also agreed that I would bring breastmilk that I expressed with a handpump in the morning and come by during my lunch break with additional breastmilk at least for the first couple of months. A was fortunate, as I had more than adequate milk. It was not difficult for me to express a bottle of milk after feeding Elizabeth in the mornings. She had already gained a lot of weight and was the most beautiful baby I had seen (I guess all mothers feel the same).

The two and a half months went fast, and it was time to go back to work.

The branch where I was going to work was on the west side of Oslo, not far from the Royal Castle and the area where my family lived before moving to Veitvet. It was also close to Oslo Handelsgym, my high school, so I knew the area well. All the embassies were located in this area, both their offices and the ambassadors' residences, and many of them were clients of the bank. With my knowledge of English, German, and French, I quickly was asked to deal with this client segment, which I enjoyed. The bank also had a number of elderly wealthy private clients who lived in the area, as well as many business clients, especially in the retail and restaurant businesses. I enjoyed the work and had interesting and nice colleagues who were a good mix of both men and women. The branch manager and his deputy and other senior staff were, however, all men.

Sometimes I half-jokingly say that I must have been sleeping when other girls and women so early realized that they did not have the same opportunities as men. I felt confident that if I worked hard and had adequate education I would be able to advance the same way as men did. So I planned to do so.

My best option was to enroll in the Norwegian Academy of Banking, which was owned by the Norwegian Bankers' Association and the Norwegian Savings Banks Association. (Today it is a part of the Norwegian Business School.) It had three levels, and you had to pass an exam from one level to advance to the next. The first and second levels were each one-year programs, while the third level, also called the higher level, was for four years. Only an exam from that level gave you the equivalent of a university degree at the intermediate level. The majority of staff members finished only the first level, and no women had attended the third level at the time.

So in September 1964, I enrolled in the Norwegian Academy of Banking. I had a full-time job and a baby, so it was important to organize my life so I could study, do the necessary homework, and still have enough time with Elizabeth. Written work had to be submitted once a month. With my high school degree, though, the subjects were comparably easy: bookkeeping, organization, Norwegian business correspondence, English business correspondence, and law. The final exams took place in June 1965, and I did well. However, I decided to wait for one year before continuing my education, as having a baby, going back to work, and studying during the same year had been a little bit tougher than I had anticipated.

We had also moved a few more times, but at last we managed to buy an apartment instead of short-term renting. We bought a one-bedroom co-op at Stabekk, just to the west of Oslo, in a nice area. We moved in just before Elizabeth turned one year, and a year later we bought a two-bedroom apartment in the same building.

When you are young, you can manage most things. In addition to work, school, household chores, and spending as much time with Elizabeth as possible, I also knitted outfits for her and sewed clothes for both of us.

And I really enjoyed it and found it relaxing. Elizabeth recently talked with me about some of those knitted outfits that she still remembers and loved very much.

I soon restarted school, and this time I knew I would have five years of schooling ahead of me. I intended to finish both the second level and higher level of the Norwegian College of Banking.

I graduated from the second level of the Norwegian College of Banking in the summer of 1967 and did very well. A few months later, my bank's director of human resources, Mr. Rasmussen, visited the branch where I worked. I had again cut my long hair a little bit, not because of the comments he had made five years earlier but rather to make it easier to manage with my hectic schedule. But he remembered and made the comment, "I like the hairstyle you have now." I decided not to respond. A few weeks later, Mr. Rasmussen called to inform me that the bank would like to offer me an interesting job, secretariat for foreign relations, at headquarters. It would be a promotion. I assumed it had to do with my performance and the additional education I had achieved and not my hairstyle, so I accepted the offer.

Th secretariat for foreign relations was a small but increasingly important part of the bank. One of its main purposes was to finance imports and exports for big customers of the bank. The bank had credit lines in foreign currency in banks worldwide, and these facilities were managed by the secretariat. We were only four in the secretariat; the other three were men, but I did exactly the same work as the others, apart from the head of the secretariat, after some training.

With my salary increase and the value of the apartment we had bought, Knut and I decided that we now could afford something bigger and better. A new development of townhouses in Asker municipality a few miles outside of Oslo had attracted our attention. Christiania Bank, like most other large banks, offered favorable mortgages to its staff members who met the necessary criteria, which I now did. I submitted my application with the necessary details. A few days later, Mr. Rasmussen called me and said he wanted to see me. He informed me that he would find it difficult to recommend the mortgage I had applied for to be granted. When I asked why, he fudged it; however, it became clear to me that it was because I was a young woman and that he did not think I would continue to work in the long run. I told him that I would then take my application to a higher level, which he did not think was a good idea. I still did. I asked for an appointment with one of the bank's executive vice presidents, Mr. Furuholmen. I had never met him before; I'd just seen him at a distance. I explained the situation. He listened carefully and informed me that a decision would be made within the next few days. A few days later, I got a letter informing me that the mortgage had been granted. I never had any problems again with loan applications.

Just after we moved to Asker, I started to be involved in local politics and got elected as a board member for the conservative party in our new district.

Christiania Bank gradually made a number of important changes both structurally and in its branding. It emerged as a more modern bank, with a new logo and new services but still with its history of the oldest commercial bank in Norway. The bank also expanded and enhanced training opportunities for staff after hiring a dynamic person as head of the newly established training and staff development department. I met him for the first time not long after he joined the bank, and he gradually became one of my most important mentors and role models. One important aspect of the bank's staff development was its own leadership development program, which it introduced in 1969. It included two years as a management trainee in key departments of the bank's headquarters and two years of theoretical studies combined with one's regular work. While I was in the middle of my studies at the third level of the Norwegian College of Banking, with the encouragement of the person in charge of the training and development department, I applied. I was one of the first twelve admitted into the program. The first two years as a trainee in key departments was relatively easy to combine with my other studies. I was the only woman among the first twelve, but later many more women were admitted. At the Norwegian College of Banking's third level, two out of the sixty-eight students who passed the final exams were women. I graduated as planned in 1971 and was then entitled to use the title "bank economist."

With my special interest in equal rights for women and men at the workplace, I started to be involved in bank employees' organizations. Over the next eight years, I went from being board member and deputy chairperson of Christiania Bank's Employees' Organization to board member of the Norwegian Society of Bank Employees in Oslo to board member of the Norwegian Union of Bank Employees. I learned at lot, including not being afraid of speaking up and also getting more women involved.

Christiania Bank, like most other banks, had gradually converted to electronically managing all client data and transactions using various computerized systems. The main conversion took place in 1966 and 1967 and had streamlined our work enormously. The bank had used a well-known company for its data processing systems; the company tailored its systems to the bank's needs. Focusing on another important part of office automation, IBM launched in 1970 the first automated word processing system. Christiania Bank was interested in exploring this, and as a part of my management trainee work in the administration and data processing department, I was asked to work on how the bank could introduce word processing in a way that could streamline all the written responses to loan applications from both private and corporate clients. This was exciting and groundbreaking. No bank in Norway had done anything like this before. While it was strongly supported by top management, it was not popular in all corners of the bank. The more senior loan officers had their own secretaries, and junior ones normally shared secretaries, so they saw this as taking something away from them and even reducing their status. Back then, every single letter was either dictated to a secretary using dictation machines or the secretary took dictation using shorthand. Some of the secretaries were not happy, while some, particularly the younger ones, saw that there could be benefits for them. So in addition to working hard on putting this project together, I also had to sell this change such that everybody would feel that they would benefit from its ability to free up time for more important work. After around three months, I finalized the project, spelling out in detail how this would work and what kind of training would be needed, both for the loan officers and for prospective staff who would be employed at the new word processing center. I also spelled out how many staff and the type of hardware we would need. With a few minor adjustments, the report and my recommendations were approved, and the word processing center was established. Since I by then had a wealth of knowledge on how this would work, top management asked me to be the manager of the center in its initial stage. I agreed. So, just before I turned twenty-seven, I became the bank's first ever female manager. As far as I know, they still have a picture of me in the bank's museum.

While I had had some great role models as leaders, they were all men. Now I had to find a style that was mine. I was not so concerned with whether my leadership style was feminine or masculine; it just had to reflect what I believed in, what I wanted to express, and how I wanted to lead. This certainly took some time, but after a year or so I was much more comfortable in my leadership position. The bank even gave me some other challenges during this period and asked me to act as a branch manager in one of the branches just outside Oslo, which gave me additional experience in leadership. I liked all of this very much.

Most people, when they get married, envisage that they will "live happily ever after." I guess I did too. While I had succeeded professionally and had been able to handle many challenges at work, I experienced problems privately that I could not handle as well. Knut was an intelligent and nice person, but he also had big internal problems. Unfortunately, he tried to deal with these problems using alcohol. The first years of our marriage, I did not understand the scope of his drinking issue, both because of my inexperience and maybe also because I was somewhat naive. While we certainly had good days, they became fewer and the problems became bigger as the years passed. I managed to convince Knut to seek professional help, which he did a few times. But it did not last long. Gradually I concentrated less on him and more on myself, my career, and my daughter. I do not regret many things in life, but I do regret that I did not ask for a divorce earlier. I think Knut, Elizabeth, and I would have been much happier, and Knut might have been forced to deal with his problems much earlier. It was only after I moved to New York that I asked for a divorce. Knut remarried a kind woman a number of years after that, and from what I heard he was happier than he had ever been in his life. Unfortunately, he passed away suddenly a few years ago, just before he turned seventy-two.

5

Onward and Upward

Every year, Christiania Bank held a meeting followed by a dinner for all the managers. The first one I attended was held just a few months after I'd been appointed manager. I still remember that I wore a black dress and put my hair, which had grown long again, up into a bun to look put together and professional. Because of my work establishing the word processing center, I knew top management very well, but many of the others I had either never met or did not know well. I was not just the only woman but also one of the youngest managers present. I could see many of the men staring and quietly saying, "Who is she? Where did she come from?" In his opening statement, the president of the bank introduced all newcomers, including me, so at least by then everybody knew who I was. After the president spoke and some of the executive vice presidents had made presentations, there was a question-and-answer session. I listened carefully and was not uniformly impressed by other managers' questions and comments. I decided not to ask questions at this meeting. However, for subsequent meetings I prepared well and always made comments and/ or asked questions.

Over the next couple of years, other banks sent people to Christiania Bank's word processing center to learn both the methodology used to establish it and how it worked in practice. Gradually, other banks would establish similar centers. It was great to be the first one, and I felt rather proud having been so instrumental in establishing it.

In addition to my full-time job, I also went through the theoretical part of Christiania Bank's leadership development program, attending seminars and lectures. In addition to top managers of Christiania Bank, they had engaged lecturers from universities, research institutions, and the private sector. I also took two languages courses, one in advanced English and one in German for bankers.

I continued to be active in Christiania Bank's employees' organization, where I was then the deputy chairperson. As mentioned previously, I was also elected as board member of the Norwegian Society of Bank Employees in Oslo.

Christiania Bank had a number of staff members from the same families working there; that also happened with our family, thanks in part to me. My brother Hans worked in the bank's mailroom for six years, until 1973, before he decided to go back to school and then to the Police Academy, after which he became a police officer. During that period, I assisted my father to get a job in the bank as well. The printing office, where he had worked for more than twenty-five years and which had been around approximately one hundred years, had struggled for a while. In 1967, another company bought it up, and all their activities moved to other premises. While my father never really complained, I was aware that he was not happy at all in this new situation. In 1971, I learned that there was an opening in the bank's supply and distribution department. I asked my father whether he would be interested, to which he said yes. I contacted the director of human resources, the relevant people met with him, and he was hired. He continued to work in the bank until he retired at the age of seventy in 1985, and he was quite happy with that. Then my youngest brother, Morten, needed a job, and with my assistance he was hired as a driver in the bank's transport and messenger department in 1984, where he stayed until 1999.

After a couple of years as head of the word processing center, I was looking for new challenges. I applied for a couple of positions in other banks, one of which I did not really want; the bank was in Alta, far up in the northern part of Norway. I applied to it, however, because they advertised that they sought a man for a general manager's position. To my big surprise, I was not only called in for interviews, but I was also apparently nominated as number two.

In May 1973, Christiania Bank was celebrating its 125th anniversary. This would be marked with two big events. The first was a black-tie dinner on the day itself, May 2, for Christiania Bank's board of directors, management, the top management of all the other banks in Norway, and representatives from other private sector companies. The other one was a grand party at the bank's headquarters for all staff in the greater Oslo area on May 5, which was a Saturday. Being a part of management, I was invited to both.

During the event on May 2, I met many people, including the Gustav Heiberg Simonsen who was the head of Bergens Kreditbank's Oslo offices. During our conversation, he told me that their present secretary to the board and administration was leaving, and because of increased workload, they had decided to establish two positions. Without promising anything, he suggested that I might consider applying for one of the positions, which would be advertised shortly. When I saw the advertisement in the newspaper, I decided to apply. I was called in for interviews with a number of people, and after a couple of months I got the exciting news that I had been selected for the job. So on September 1, 1973, I joined Bergens Kreditbank in Oslo as one of their two secretaries to the board and administration.

Bergens Kreditbank's headquarters was in Bergen, Norway's second largest city, on the west coast of Norway. The city is around one thousand years old and has always been an important city in trade.

Bergens Kreditbank was originally established in 1859 as a branch of Christiania Bank, but it became an independent bank in 1876. It entered into problems in the early 1920s and was then reestablished in the same premises in 1928.

When I joined the office in Oslo in 1973, it was flourishing under the dynamic leadership of Gustav Heiberg Simonsen. He was only in his late thirties but had already acquired a lot of banking experience. He had also practiced as a lawyer on cases for the supreme curt.

I liked the people I worked with and enjoyed my work. My responsibilities were to prepare and analyze all the material and cases that were to be presented to the board for decision and to prepare the cases that were to be decided by the administration of Bergens Kreditbank in Oslo. My responsibilities included affairs related to both private and corporate clients, and I had frequent meetings with some of the large corporate clients. The board meetings took place on a rotating basis in Oslo and

Bergen, and from time to time I traveled to Bergen to attend the board meetings there.

In 1975, the respective boards of Bergens Kreditbank and Bergens Privatbank, the latter a much larger bank that also had its headquarters in Bergen and a large office in Oslo, decided to merge. This decision, as always in a merger, had an impact on all of us, particularly those of us coming from the smaller of the two banks. Top management from both banks negotiated the positions, which I am sure was not easy. On paper, I got a great position in the new bank, which was called Bergen Bank. I was a manager responsible for the bank's branches in Oslo, reporting to the person who had been my boss in Bergens Kreditbank, whom I respected and liked at lot.

While my salary was good and the position sounded nice, I realized after a while that the job was neither challenging nor something I would be satisfied with in the long run. I had to do something else. In the meantime, I continued my involvement in bank employees' organizations and was elected board member of Norwegian Union of Bank Employees, which covers employees in all the banks in Norway. My involvement in these organizations gave me experience working on a number of staff-related issues, particularly equality for women at the workplace, as well as experience and confidence in public speaking.

After a year or so, I saw an opportunity. A position at Bergen Bank's office in Sandvika, which is the administrative center of the municipality of Bærum, approximately 15 kilometers (9.3 miles) west of Oslo, was advertised internally. The post was for a manager who would be responsible for the credit and loan area as well as for some of the marketing and public relations for the office. The position could be seen as a step down from what I had at the headquarters in Oslo, but I did not care: I would rather have a position that was interesting and challenging than something that was just prestigious on paper. I discussed this with the director for human resources, who arranged for an interview with the general manager for Bergen Bank in Sandvika. I got the job and started the first working day in January 1977. I was thrilled with this decision.

While I enjoyed both work and the working environment, I decided to apply for another job in another bank after a year. The bank was called Kjøbmandsbanken, which means "the Merchant's Bank," an independent medium-sized commercial bank in Oslo that was established in 1913. While the bank had a number of private customers, their customer base consisted mostly of small and medium-sized corporate customers. The position was assistant general manager and entailed being responsible for credits and loans, investments, marketing, and especially on increasing the bank's customer base.

I was called in for interviews not only with the general manager but also with the entire board of directors. The interviews went well, and after a couple of months I was informed that I had been selected for the job.

While the job itself was fascinating, I found after a while that the general manager and the board were very conservative and somewhat old-fashioned in their thinking. They were not especially open for new ideas and out-of-the-box approaches. So, when after around two years I saw Christiania Bank advertising for an assistant general manager at their office in Sandvika, Bærum, the same place where I had earlier worked for Bergen Bank, I decided to apply.

Christiania Bank's office in Bærum was one of its largest offices outside of Oslo. In addition to its main office in Sandvika, it also had a number of branches in other parts of Bærum. The office, like all other offices of Christiania Bank outside of Oslo, had its own board of directors.

I got the job. The general manager was a great person to work with. He was open to more women being promoted into higher-lever positions, and within a year the office had three women at managerial levels and a few more in senior officer positions. He also encouraged me to be active in the local business association. I became a board member of Bærum Business Association and, a couple of years later, its chairperson. I had also been asked by the Ministry of Foreign Affairs whether I would be interested in becoming a deputy representative in the Advisory Committee for Cooperation with Developing Countries in the Petroleum Sector, which I accepted. After a year in the office, I was promoted to deputy general manager.

While bank robberies in Norway at the time were rare, banks had started to increase security. Christiania Bank's headquarters had established a security department, and large offices like Christiania Bank in Bærum, which had a number of branches, had hired their own security officers. Each officer made sure office routines were safe and that all staff underwent training twice a year so that everybody would know what to do in the event of a security incident, including a possible bank robbery.

And then it happened. One morning, my phone rang. It was one of our branch managers. His message was clear: they'd had a bank robbery, and one of their staff members had been critically wounded and another taken hostage. The bank robber had entered the bank just after they'd opened with a sawed-off shotgun, demanded money, and asked the staff to get down on the floor. When the robber felt that one of the staff members—the deputy branch manager—was too slow, he fired several shots, some of which hit the staff member in one of his lungs and one arm. The branch manager had done all the correct things that we had gone through during the training. The staff member had been taken to the hospital for emergency surgery, and the police were already there. I told him I would be there shortly, together with our security officer. My assistant said later that she knew something was wrong when she saw me running out of my office toward the security officer's office; I normally walked fast but would never run.

On this particular day, the entire top management of Christiania Bank, including the general manager of the office in Bærum, was attending a strategy meeting at a hotel outside of Oslo, so I was really on my own to try to make all the right decisions. There were many, and I had to make them fast. First, it was important that the injured staff member's wife be informed. She worked in another branch in Oslo, and I asked the security officer immediately to call that branch manager so he could inform her and escort her to the hospital to see her husband. Then I had to call the general manager of Christiania Bank in Bærum. He was shocked and asked whether I needed any help, but I said I was able to manage. He would call me back regularly for updates and would inform the members of top management who were at the hotel with him.

It turned out that the staff member who had been taken hostage had been asked by the bank robber to use his car to drive him where he wanted to go, under the threat that he would shoot him if he refused. Luckily, the bank robber at some stage asked him to stop the car and to leave. He managed to alert the police, and while he was traumatized, he was otherwise okay. All the staff members were traumatized. I contacted the regional hospital for advice on what could be done for the staff. The only advice I got was to tell them to take a sleeping pill before going to bed. I knew that they would need more than that. I remembered reading not long before this happened about a psychologist from Oslo who had done trauma counseling after a major accident had happened in Norway. I called the regional hospital again, both to find out how our staff member was doing and to ask their help in finding this psychologist. Our staff member was still in critical condition, and the hospital indicated that they might have to amputate a part of his left arm. They told me they would do their utmost to find the psychologist, which they did. She would make herself available for staff counseling both individually and in groups from the following day. And then there was the media. A large number of television and print media organizations were camping outside the bank branch. I went out to talk to them, gave them the basic information, and asked for their understanding; we had a staff member in critical condition, and the rest of the staff members were traumatized. I told them I would give them an update the following day if they wished.

We assisted the staff members as they left, whether in their own car, a relative's car, or by taxi, by making sure they were not bothered by the media. After that and after the police had taken the necessary evidence, fingerprints etc., the security officer and I arranged for somebody to come clean up as much as possible. There was a lot of blood around, and we wanted it to be removed and cleaned up before staff returned the following they. Afterward, we went to the hospital to meet with the injured staff member's wife and to find out how he was doing. He was still in serious condition.

The following week I returned to the branch every day, both to show support to the staff members who remarkably came to work every day and to respond to the media. The suspected bank robber, a twenty-five-year-old man, was arrested and eventually confessed. Our staff member improved, but unfortunately they had to amputate a part of his arm, as feared. He later came back to work for a while but suffered a lot from phantom pain in the part of the arm that had been amputated. He later decided to take an early retirement package that the bank offered him.

Both the general manager and the top management at Christiania Bank''s headquarters told me that they were very pleased with the way I had handled this extremely challenging situation.

In early 1982, I received a phone call from the office of one of the bank's executive vice presidents. He wanted to meet with me later that week. I was curious what this was all about. When I met with him, he told me that the bank's top management wanted to offer me the position of senior vice president and head of marketing and product development at the bank's headquarters. Of course I was interested, and I accepted on the spot. I also knew that this would be challenging. This was the first time any bank had appointed a woman as senior vice president at its headquarters in Oslo, so again I made history, and I did so before I turned forty.

Christiania Bank had merged less than two years before with another fairly large bank, Andresen's Bank, a bank mostly based in Oslo, and some of the staff in the marketing and product development division came from Andresen's Bank. I knew a few of them, particularly from courses I had attended under the auspices of the Norwegian Bankers' Association. The staff in the division ranged in age from twenty-five to sixty, with a good mix of men and women but again with more men than women in senior positions.

While I was familiar with all types of accounts and services the bank had to offer, both in private retail banking as well as in the business sector, and while marketing had been one of my responsibilities as deputy general manager, this was still a different world. We were working on new products to increase our market shares, which was fascinating. And then there were relationships with advertising agencies so we could best promote our services through advertising campaigns, which I had never been involved in before. We had extensive brainstorming sessions both internally and with the advertising companies. These companies were even more male-dominated than banking, and I realized soon that gender equality was not on their agenda. While I always tried to reach a consensus, particularly internally, the final decision would most of the time rest with me, while major changes had to go to the executive vice president for approval.

In addition to my exciting work, I added a lot of other things to my increasingly expanding agenda. It started when the top management in Christiania Bank supported my request to attend the most prestigious executive leadership program in Norway, a nine-week course at the Administrative Research Institute at the Norwegian School of Economics in Bergen. The course was divided into three three-week seminars in a hotel just outside of Bergen. The participants all had reached various leadership positions already; they were a diverse group from the military, public, and private sectors. The majority of the participants were men, but there were a few women as well. The course was intense but rewarding. A year or so later, I also became a board member of the Administrative Research Institute.

When ordinary people started to travel abroad again after the Second World War, particularly from 1960 onward, credit cards were not used much for private travel in Europe. The use of traveler's checks was much more common. A company called Euro Travellers Cheque International had been established mid-1960 with its headquarters in Brussels, Belgium. A large number of banks bought their traveler's checks and related services from that company, particularly for use in Europe. Other traveler's checks, like American Express, were also available. The company had a board consisting mostly of representatives from bank associations in Europe. Norwegian banks had one representative on the board from the Norwegian Bankers' Association. When the present Norwegian representative was leaving, the Norwegian Bankers' Association contacted Christiania Bank's management to find out whether I would be interested in replacing him. The management was thrilled with this, and I accepted. It was an unpaid board directorship, but the company paid for travel and accommodations to support my attendance at board meetings. While many board meetings were held at the headquarters in Brussels, some meetings were held in truly fascinating places, such as Monte Carlo, St. Moritz, Paris, and London. I still remember vividly a board meeting that took place in Monte Carlo. After the meeting and after dinner, a few of us decided to visit the casino. Some had been there before, but it was my first time. The casino had a number of rooms, including a room with the slot machines; the placement of the rooms seemed to depend on the importance of and, I guess, money involved in the game. I played on the slot machines for a while, having decided I could spend fifty francs. I won a little bit and lost a little bit and stopped after a while. One of the board members who apparently knew the casino well wanted to take me to the most inner room to show me something. There was a not-so-young woman in the room. I still remember her long, thin fingers with several diamond rings. She was playing on the roulette. After a while, one of the servants came with a silver tray holding a glass of water and a couple of tablets. The woman took the tablets and swallowed them with the water and then gave the servant a big tip. The person from the board who had accompanied me said that he had seen the woman several times there. He had been told that she was extremely rich but living alone with her household staff and that the only thing she did was to come to the casino every evening to play a little bit and have some company. He had also been told that she had to take some medication and that the staff in the casino was almost fighting over who should bring it to her because she always gave a big tip. I felt very sad seeing the woman. She had all of this money but no family that cared about her, and she had to go to the casino to pay for company and to feel that somebody cared about her.

The first board meeting I attended, however, took place in Brussels. Documents were mailed in advance. I read everything carefully and prepared myself thoroughly. When the meeting started, I saw one of the other board members, all men apart from me, opening the envelope with the documents at the meeting itself. He had apparently not bothered to read any of the documents. I thought to myself that only a man would do that and not feel ashamed.

Sometimes there is an advantage to being a woman, particularly if you are well educated and have financial experience. Companies and/ or organizations with governing entities might seek for you to join their membership. That happened to me as well. I was contacted by the Norway's Ministry of Finance to see whether I would be its representative in the corporate assembly of the state-owned coal-mining company, Store Norske Spitsbergen Kulkompani, which was and still is the northernmost mining company in the world. It is located in Svalbard, the archipelago in the Arctic Ocean that falls midway between continental Norway and the North Pole. While there had been daily flights between Tromsø on mainland Norway to Spitsbergen, the largest of the islands, there were no regular hotel accommodations. Today a number of tourists go to Svalbard, where there are now a few hotels and guesthouses, and tours are arranged for tourists. Tourism has now become an important supplementary industry there. This responsibility was something exciting that I did not mind doing. I was informed that members of the corporate assembly go to Svalbard twice a year on inspection tours, in October/November and in May/June.

I did not know a lot about Svalbard aside from the limited knowledge I had from geography, history lessons at school, and the newspaper articles that had covered a big mining accident there around twenty years earlier. The ministry sent me, however, piles of documents—background documents about Svalbard and documents about the company's past and present. From these, I learned the following: Administratively, the archipelago is not part of any Norwegian county but rather forms an unincorporated area administered by a state-appointed governor. The Svalbard Treaty of 1920 recognizes Norwegian sovereignty, and the 1925 Svalbard Act made Svalbard a full part of the Kingdom of Norway. However, all signatories to the treaty were granted nondiscriminatory rights to fishing, hunting, and mineral resources. Both during the years when I was a member of the corporate assembly and today, the only country in addition to Norway that has taken advantage of this is Russia (which was still the Soviet Union when I was there). During the time I was there, the Russian population at Svalbard was as large as or slightly larger than the Norwegian population (around 2,400 to 2,500 of each nationality), but today, from what I understand, the Russian population is much smaller.

During my visits over the next three years, I experienced both the polar night, when it is dark both during the day and night, and the midnight sun, when the sun never sets. The polar night lasts from around October 20 to February 20, and the midnight sun lasts from around April 20 to August 20. I did, however, experience some light when I visited during the polar night due to the full moon reflecting off of the snow.

The visits were really extraordinary experiences that I am so happy I had. As I mentioned, there were no hotels, so we stayed in the accommodations built for employees in the company's official representation building. The building had been built in 1947 and had wonderful views of Longyearbyen (Longyear Town), the administrative center of Svalbard, the Lars glacier, and the Longyear glacier.

The administrative center, Longyearbyen, is named after John Munro Longyear, whose Arctic Coal Company started coal mining operations in 1906. This was taken over by Store Norske Spitsbergen Kulkompani later.

During my visits, we had to inspect coalmines, which involved crawling in narrow mines and walking in bigger ones. We had to get extensive security briefings before each coal-mining visit and had to put on special outfits. I could easily see how difficult and often dangerous that work is. We also visited Barentsburg, which is the place inhabited by Russians. Interestingly, they used Moscow time (which is two hours ahead of Norwegian time), while the rest of Svalbard used Norwegian time. We also went on snowmobiles, a popular mode of transportation. A few of the people accompanying us on these trips always had to carry rifles as a last resort in case we encountered polar bears that attacked. I saw these impressive creatures once, a polar bear and her cub, while still a distance away. They started to move toward us, and we all were relieved when they decided to turn around and move away. Svalbard has mostly permafrost, with some areas of tundra, but it also has interesting flora that take advantage of the long periods of midnight sun. I was always amazed to see beautiful flowers coming up through the snow during my May/June visits.

1983 was the year for local government elections in Norway. While I had been involved in local politics before, I had never wanted to run for office. During one of the Conservative meetings I participated in in Oslo, I was asked whether I could spend some weekends campaigning leading up to the election. Some of the board members suggested that my name should be on the list of candidates in a place where I would have the opportunity to be elected as a member of the City Council of Oslo. If elected as deputy member, it would most likely be far down on the list—meaning, I would be elected to a post with limited responsibility. That suited me well since I had more than enough on my plate already. It was interesting to spend some weekends standing on street corners with other members of the Conservative Party, speaking with and answering questions from the public. The election took place in September, and in Oslo the Conservative Party won with a small majority. The system of election in Norway is that people who vote can change the order of the prospective candidates on a party list. This time voters were particularly encouraged to move women further up on the list. While I was not among the twenty-six members from the Conservative Party elected, I had been moved much further up, so I was elected as third deputy member of the City Council. The implications were that I would have to meet in the City Council often. It also opened a floodgate. I had to turn down the many invitations that soon followed from other committees or boards that sought my involvement either as a member or deputy member, but I did accept to be a deputy member of the Oslo Electricity Company, which provided electricity to the entire city of Oslo, as well as the Industrial and Employment Board of the City of Oslo. These were fascinating experiences.

In the fall of 1983, the boards of Christiania Bank and Fiskernes Bank (which means "the Fishermen's Bank") decided to merge. The official date for the merger was set to May 2, 1984. Fiskernes Bank had its headquarters in Tromsø, with a number of branches along the coastline of the northern part of Norway. Tromsø is the largest city in the northern part of Norway and is located 350 kilometers (around 210 miles) north of the Arctic Circle. I was asked to be a part of the transition team, and over the next six months, from November 1983 to April 2, 1984, I went to Fiskernes Bank's headquarters or to one of their branches every second week for a couple of days. While I had experienced both polar nights and the midnight sun before during my trips to Svalbard, this was different since I was going to the northern part of Norway quite often. I guess one needs to be born in this part of the world to deal with the polar nights in particular. While the days are short during part of the winter in Oslo, we still have some sun, but in the north one did not, which can be quite depressing. While the real midnight sun period started just after my biweekly trips ended, the twilight period lasts a long time, so there is really no darkness during it. It was not uncommon to see people, for example, painting their houses during late-night hours.

To promote the "new" bank, we decided to invite a number of journalists to Svolvær, in the Lofoten archipelago, where great cod fishing takes place from January to late March every year. The cod fisheries were and still are an important foundation for the town. The idea was for me to take the journalists out early in the morning for around six hours with one of the fishing boats so we could experience the fishing, and then we had invited one of the most well-known chefs at that time to make a variety of dishes from the cod and present them to us all for dinner. In the early morning we went out with the fishing boat, and the weather was terrible—there was rain and wind, and the sea was high. The manager of Fiskernes Bank in Svolvær, who was born there, said he was not going out.

The fishermen said it would be okay, and most of the journalists and I braved it and went out. I do not easily get seasick, and I did not this time either, but I was relieved when we got back on land after five or six hours. I still have a diploma certifying that I went cod fishing in Lofoten on March 21, 1984. The chef and his team had already started to prepare some of the cod dishes when we returned, and he also got some of the cod from our trip. The variety of the dishes was fantastic. The journalists had a lot of pictures taken and did some nice write-ups, and we all enjoyed a fabulous dinner. The next day, the weather was fantastic—sunny and beautiful. I was sorry that was not the day we had planned to go fishing!

For many years I had been involved in issues related to gender equality and women in the workplace both through my engagement with employees' organizations and in the various banks I had worked in. I had been a speaker on these issues in a number of meetings for a variety of organizations, including the Rotary Club at a time when they still did not allow women to become members. When Christiania Bank decided in 1980 to establish its Gender Equality Committee, I was not surprised to be asked to be one of its members. While we had many tense discussions, I would certainly give the bank's top management a lot of credit for their openness to addressing complex issues. The first action program was presented and agreed upon in early 1981, with targets to be achieved for numbers and percentages of women over the next three years. Three years later, the targets had almost been achieved at all levels, and new and higher targets were agreed upon with a new action program. I often had tough discussions about these issues with the director for human resources, a retired army major. We had not always been in agreement. For that reason, it was particularly touching when, in addition to the official letter Christiana Bank sent me when I made my final decision to leave, he sent me a personal note, thanking me for my good cooperation over many years. He added that while we maybe at the outset had different views on women's situations in the bank, he felt that we gradually had come to good terms with each other.

6

UNICEF

To write about my years with UNICEF could be a book by itself, and I do not intend to write that book. However, I spent more than nineteen years working for UNICEF, so of course I have to mention some elements of that time in my life. The first chapter of this book describes my first couple of years in the organization, including my first fieldtrip, so this chapter will concentrate on many other aspects of my time with UNICEF.

To work for UNICEF changed my life in many ways. It gave me opportunities that I never thought I would get, including to contribute to the improvement of the world's children in more ways than I had ever envisioned. It also gave me the opportunity to travel to a large number of countries; during my nineteen-plus years with UNICEF, I traveled to more than one hundred countries, many of them a number of times. I saw a lot of positive developments, but I also witnessed terrible situations for children.

UNICEF was established as a temporary emergency organization on December 10, 1946, to assist children in war-torn Europe after the Second World War. After a few years, when the situation for children in Europe improved but so many challenges were affecting children in the developing world, UNICEF became a permanent organization of the United Nations system.

When I joined UNICEF, about 14 million children under the age of five were dying every year in the developing world, most of them from easily preventable diseases, in what Jim Grant, UNICEF's executive director, called "silent emergencies." He had launched an initiative called "The Child Survival and Development Revolution."

Jim Grant was a unique person in many ways. He was born in China in 1922, the son of a well-known public health specialist who was committed to healthcare for all in China. He believed healthcare should be inexpensive enough for the working class to afford; that it should focus on preventive care, such as health promotion, nutrition improvement, and hygiene improvement; and that it should use health workers recruited from the community. I was told that Jim Grant, from an early age, often accompanied his father on field trips and that this had a major impact on his views and approaches later in life.

After he joined UNICEF as its executive director, he proposed that the organization should assist countries in reducing early childhood diseases using simple techniques. In the area of primary health care, four practices were singled out and referred to as "GOBI": *G* stood for "growth monitoring," which should be used to monitor child well-being; *O* stood for "oral rehydration therapy," which should be used to reduce the impact of childhood diarrhea; *B* stood for "breastfeeding" and included the need for a nutritional start in life; and *I* stood for "immunization against vaccine-preventable childhood diseases."

A few years earlier, I had listened to a lecture about leadership at a seminar in Norway. The person who gave the lecture said, among other things, "A good leader is a person who can motivate ordinary people to make an extraordinary effort in achieving things." Jim Grant was that kind of leader. He could convince most people, from UNICEF staff to presidents or prime ministers, to take actions to make a difference for children in the world.

As one of the three deputy executive directors in UNICEF, I had the responsibility to oversee operations, including human resources, accounts, finance, budget, IT, and supply and procurement. I met with each of the directors reporting to me individually once a week, unless I was traveling. Sometimes we met as a group, and from time to time I attended their staff meetings so I could meet with all staff. However, I got involved in so many UNICEF activities, directly and indirectly, that when I traveled to country offices I represented UNICEF in all its aspects, both in internal discussions and in discussions with government and NGO partners. I have met numerous presidents and prime ministers from around the world, but the meetings with ordinary people, in particular women and children, were what mattered most. Being a woman myself, I could more easily talk with women and understand many of their issues, including their fears and frustrations and their hopes and aspirations.

One of my early travels to Africa took me to Mali, in West Africa. Like a few other countries in West Africa, Mali was recovering from an emergency situation caused by a long draught. Mali also had one of the highest child mortality rates in the world. The literacy rate was low: only 23 percent of men and 16 percent of women were literate.

I arrived in the capital, Bamako, at night after a long trip from New York via Brussels. The next morning would be exciting, as I was going to Timbuktu. For me, Timbuktu had always been something mythical, and a very faraway place. We would fly to Timbuktu the next morning on a small plane that seated five passengers. The plane was operated by an NGO, and the pilots were off-duty Air France pilots volunteering their services. I remember thinking that it must have been very different to fly a Boeing 747 or a DC-10 than such a small, not-so-sophisticated plane. We had to stop once in Gao to refuel before we got to Timbuktu.

From the material I had received, I learned that Timbuktu had become a permanent settlement in the twelfth century and had flourished from trade. It had also been known for an important Islamic university which attracted scholars from throughout the Islamic world and was a center in Africa. Different tribes had governed Timbuktu until 1893 when it was formally incorporated into the French colony of Mali. In 1960 it became a part of the Republic of Mali when the country achieved its independence.

When I visited Timbuktu, it had a high poverty level, and children's health and education were dramatically inadequate. Only 35 percent of boys and 16 percent of girls enrolled in primary school, and of those who enrolled, only around 60 percent finished. The recent extensive drought had not made either health or education conditions any better. One of the big challenges was access to clean water. I visited the health clinic for mothers and children and saw how they tried to assist children using ORS (oral rehydration therapy) who had been dehydrated from diarrhea. The mothers I met had the same aspirations for their children as mothers and fathers have all over the world: they wanted their children to be safe and happy and to grow up healthy and strong.

While French was and is the official language in Mali, the majority of the population spoke a local language, which some mixed with Arabic and some mixed with French. I saw, however, a teacher sitting with children under a tree and writing in French in beautiful cursive on a blackboard. The teacher was having the children repeat the words and write them on a piece of paper. I wondered whether this was the most effective way to improve the children's education.

Timbuktu had no hotels when I was there, and we were going to stay in somebody's house. It was uncomfortably hot, so someone decided that our hosts would put mattresses on the flat roof, and we would all sleep up there. A wonderful meal had been prepared of grilled lamb with couscous and red wine. We all slept well; the night was reasonably cool, and the sky was clear and full of stars. It was as magical as I thought Timbuktu would be. But the next day was quite different. We experienced a sandstorm in which we had to cover our heads and parts of our faces with scarves. The pilot told us that we could not return to Bamako as planned and would have to wait until the sandstorm was over. In the late afternoon, the weather had improved enough to take off, but it was a bumpy trip. I sat next to the pilot, which was exciting. After one stop to refuel, we all arrived safely in Bamako.

UNICEF was governed by an executive board representing member states of the United Nations. Until 1994, it consisted of forty-one members, which was then reduced to thirty-six. The members were elected on a regional basis for three years. Any member state of the United Nations could, however, meet as an observer during the years they were not members of the UNICEF Executive Board. Each member state, whether full member or observer, attended the board with a delegation of several members, so depending on what was discussed, there could be two hundred to two hundred and fifty people present at any time. When the board was reduced from forty-one to thirty-six members in 1994, a number of other changes also took place. Until then, there had been one board meeting that lasted for two weeks once a year in April, with individual meetings lasting sometimes until after midnight. It was like running a marathon. Starting in 1994, there were two or three regular board meetings and one annual meeting a year, and the time was more or less kept to normal hours in a slightly more businesslike manner.

Sitting up at the podium and having to answer questions from board members was interesting to say the least. I always tried to do it in a calm, precise way, even when I found some of the questions irrelevant and/or nitpicky.

In my office in UNICEF House, I had a few important quotes framed on the wall. They are now on the wall in my home office. One of them was a quote by Albert Einstein: "In a moment of crisis, imagination is as important as knowledge." I often looked at the quote before deciding what to do in a challenging situation. And the challenges were many, both on the program side and the operation side. On the operation side, which was my area of responsibility, the executive board sometimes wanted to micromanage things. For example, they tried to micromanage issues related to our move to new premises, which we would rent. The new building was under construction when I joined UNICEF, and we moved into it in August 1987. The building, which was on Forty-Fourth Street between First and Second Avenues, just across the street from the UN Headquarters, would be named UNICEF House. UNICEF would be responsible for the one-time installation costs, which is where the board came in. They concerned themselves with everything from how many bathrooms it would have to what the cafeteria would be like to, of course, how much money would be spent. After many meetings and reviews, these particular issues were finally settled. But there were many other issues over the years—some of them relevant and serious, and some not—and they were all time-consuming.

I met so many wonderful people working for UNICEF over the years I was there. Many of them became friends—some of them close friends. One person who became a special friend early was Michael Shower. He had joined UNICEF in 1980, when Jim Grant became the executive director; they working closely. Mike was on the one hand an introvert, and on the other hand he was a brilliant, passionate, strategic thinker who had a vision for what UNICEF could and should do to improve children's situations around the world. He and Jim Grant were a powerful team. Mike did not warm up to people fast, but for some interesting reasons, we fast became close friends. Mike was openly gay, and his partner had died from AIDS just a few months before I'd joined UNICEF. Mike was himself HIV positive and started to take AZT, the first medication for HIV/AIDS. It came on the market in 1987, and though it was not a cure, it would slow down the development of full-blown AIDS. He was open about this. Mike lived in a top-floor apartment in Greenwich Village in New York, and I was often there. I spent Fourths of July, Thanksgivings, and New Year's Days with him, and he always had wonderful parties with interesting guests.

In October 1988, the UN General Assembly approved, after it had been worked on and lobbied for for a year or so, that December 1 every year would be commemorated as World Aids Day. On December 1, 1988, the first World Aids Day was commemorated in many parts of the world, including at the UN Headquarters in New York. In 1987, Mike had met Cleve Jones, an American AIDS activist who conceived of the idea of the Names Project AIDS Memorial Quilt that would have panels of names of people who had died from AIDS. Mike got the idea that the quilt should be displayed at this first World AIDS Day at the United Nations, and he succeeded. He also succeeded in getting Cleve Jones to attend and to speak about the origin of the quilt. Today the Names Project AIDS Memorial Quilt has become at fifty-four tons, the world's largest piece of community folk art. Mike Shower asked me in advance to participate, which I willingly did. It was a moving ceremony that entailed remembering those who had died from AIDS and focusing on what could be done to prevent HIV/AIDS from spreading. Five of us read pieces to remember people who had died from AIDS. I read about a woman and her son from New York. Her husband had infected her, and she had transmitted it to her son when he was born. Every December 1, World Aids Day continues to be commemorated around the world, with a different thematic focus each time. In 1988, the theme was communication, which continues to be essential.

Two other people I became close friends with early on are Mehr Khan and her husband, John Williams. When I first met them, John, an Australian, was the director of the Division of Information, and Mehr, a Pakistani, was a senior officer in the Programme Funding Office, dealing with government funding. They had both been married before. I remember when they married each other in the early part of 1986, as I was at their dinner reception. They are still happily married today. We often had dinner together when I was at UNICEF, most of the time in their apartment, where Mehr made fantastic Pakistani dishes, and occasionally at my place. We have continued to be close friends, which I am thrilled about, and I consider them special and important people in my life.

In 1979, the UN General Assembly adopted CEDAW, the Convention on Elimination of All Forms of Discrimination against Women. This focus on women's rights also increased the pressure to recognize the rights of children and highlighted the need to have a convention on children's rights to replace the 1959 Declaration of the Rights of the Child. In particular, NGOs working on children's issues assisted in establishing an intergovernmental group under the UN Commission on Human Rights in 1979, after the International Year of the Child. In 1987, as I remember very well, Jim Grant said that the movement for children's rights, and the convention for children, would be critical for UNICEF's work with governments to expand the child survival and development revolution. He also said that he had decided to put a number of key staff members in Geneva to work on the drafting of the Convention of the Rights of the Child. This advanced quickly. Two years later, on November 20, 1989, thirty years after the 1959 Declaration of the Rights of the Child, the UN General Assembly adopted the Convention of the Rights of the Child. It was an exciting day for UNICEF, for everybody who had worked so hard to make this happen, and most importantly, for the children of the world. I remember it as if it were today: I was sitting in the General Assembly Hall in the area designated for senior UN officials. In the first row were Jim Grant; Jan Mårtenson, undersecretary general for human rights and head of the UN office in Geneva; and Audrey Hepburn, goodwill ambassador for UNICEF. Behind them sat a number of key UNICEF staff members, including myself.

I had met Audrey Hepburn in 1988 when she became a UNICEF goodwill ambassador just before her first trip for UNICEF to Somalia. When she returned from Somalia, she was going to have a press briefing in UNICEF House. To prepare herself, she was sitting in the conference room outside my office going through her notes, which were all handwritten. I went to say hello and asked whether she wanted her notes typed up. She smiled a beautiful warm smile and said she preferred her own handwritten notes, as they were all in big letters so that she would not have to wear glasses. I invited her into my office for a cup of coffee. I was a little surprised that she looked somewhat tense; I never thought an experienced movie star would be nervous about speaking to media, so I asked whether there was anything else I could do for her.

She looked at me and said, "Is there anywhere here where I can have a cigarette? That would really help me. I don't smoke much anymore, but right now I really need a cigarette."

When we moved into UNICEF House in 1987, Jim Grant had decided that smoking would not be allowed in any office. He designated two smoking rooms for those who really needed a cigarette. Being a smoker myself back then, I had gone to one of the smoking rooms once, but I could not stand the heavy smoke and smell and never returned, which curtailed my habit. I eventually stopped smoking entirely in 1989. I didn't think taking Audrey Hepburn to one of the smoking rooms was an option, so I decided that I would allow her to smoke in my office and take the blame if discovered. I told my assistant that I would close the door and that we should not be disturbed. One needed a special key to unlock any of the windows, which I had. So I opened the window and told her that she could have her cigarette in my office. I still had an ashtray, now used only for decoration, which came in handy. She was so grateful and happy and much more relaxed. The press briefing was a great success.

Every time Audrey Hepburn visited UNICEF House in New York and I was there, she would come by the office to say hello. A few times in life one is fortunate to meet a person like Audrey; she was beautiful outside and inside, and she worked so hard in her capacity as a goodwill ambassador for UNICEF, particularly on behalf of children in very difficult circumstances. Late in 1992, I remember Audrey was back from a trip to the Sudan. I was in a meeting when my assistant passed me a note that Audrey Hepburn was outside the meeting room just wanting to say hello. I went outside. I found her looking tired but did not think too much about it since I knew the trip had been a tough one. She gave me a hug and said that she did not want to leave without saying hello to me. Little did I know that that would be the last time I would see Audrey. Not long after she returned to Switzerland, where she lived, she was hospitalized and passed away from cancer in January 1993.

Jim Grant wanted more for children in the world. He wanted to create a political will by presidents and prime ministers worldwide to commit themselves to clear goals and targets for the improvement of the lives of children. He wanted them all to come together to talk about what could and should be done. And in his 1989 annual report, *State of the World's Children*, which was launched in December 1988, he posed this question: hasn't the time come to have all heads of state or government meeting and committing to concrete goals regarding the survival, development, and protection of children? Jim Grant himself would, of course, do the main launch of the report. I had, however, been asked to go to Stockholm, Sweden, for a side launch, which I did with Lisbeth Palme, the wife of the late prime minister of Sweden, Oluf Palme, who had been assassinated in early 1988. She was the chairperson of the Swedish National Committee for UNICEF. The exciting thing was that the minister of development cooperation, who also attended the press conference, read a letter from the prime minister of Sweden, Ingvar Carlson, that said that he fully agreed with Jim Grant: the time had come to have a meeting at the top level to discuss and focus on the issue of children, and he continued saying, "and I will personally like to be involved in that." Jim Grant managed to get another five presidents or prime minister to endorse his call and assert willingness to be involved. They were Prime Minister Brian Mulroney of Canada, President Hosni Mubarak of Egypt, President Moussa Traore of Mali, President Carlos Salinas de Gortari of Mexico, and Prime Minister Benazir Bhutto of Pakistan. These six countries and their heads of government would be the organizers of the World Summit for Children, and UNICEF would act as the secretariat.

Over the next eighteen months or so, Jim Grant managed what most other people thought was impossible. The obstacles were many, from the seating around the table in the ECOSOC Chamber of the UN to how many minutes each head of state or government would speak—and, of course, he had to figure out how many would attend at that level. The permanent representatives to the UN and other staff from the organizer countries formed a committee working with UNICEF and the UN system to assist with ironing out all the challenges. Prime Minister Brian Mulroney and President Moussa Traore would co-chair the meeting. Jim Grant managed to convince both president George H. W. Bush and Prime

Minister Margaret Thatcher to attend just before the meeting. A total of seventy-one heads of state or government had agreed to attend, the largest number of heads of state or government to attend a meeting up to that point. An additional eighty-eight observers, most of them at the ministerial level, had also confirmed their attendance.

One big challenge, as mentioned above, was how long the seventy-one heads of state could be allowed to speak. In UN meetings, there was normally no time limit for speeches by heads of state. But this was different. The meeting was only going to last for one day, so all had to be accommodated within that day. Fortunately, this was not a UN meeting; it was a meeting organized by six member states. After difficult negotiations, it was finally decided that the maximum speaking time for each head of state or government would be five minutes. That meant that there would be no time for other speakers, not even Jim Grant, which from his and UNICEF's point of view was not acceptable. After another round of negotiations, Jim Grant was allocated four minutes to address the world leaders at the opening of the meeting. But it was so hard to limit what Jim wanted to convey to four minutes. Then the idea came up to have a video made, and it was eventually agreed that the video could be twelve minutes. The video was called "341," named after the number of children under five years of age who would die, most of them from preventable diseases, during the twelve minutes of the video. It was screened at the opening of the meeting, together with Jim Grant's opening speech, and was also shown on television stations in around ninety countries worldwide the same day.

Everything else had to be planned in great detail, from the picture of all the heads of state that had to be taken just before the meetings started, to how to get all the heads of state and government into the UN premises on time, to how the security would work with so many high-level people coming at one time. The issues were almost too numerous to list. For the picture, we had UNICEF staff members whose heights resembled those of the heads of state and government to line up (I still have that picture), and then each space was marked so it would be easy to get the heads of state in the right spot fast. A breakfast meeting would start in the delegates' lounge at seven o'clock in the morning, and we had staggered the heads of state to arrive with one minute between each motorcade (we had a number of dry runs); they had to arrive exactly at the time given. Some, with the clearance of their own security people, preferred to walk from the hotel where they were staying to the UN premises, as this meant they could come at any time as long as they arrived before the meeting started.

I remember very well the day before the World Summit for Children. Jim Grant had asked me to meet with Queen Noor of Jordan. Her husband, the King, unfortunately was not able to attend, so she was going to be there in his stead. She was staying at the Waldorf Astoria, where the meeting was set to take place. I had already met Queen Noor a month or so earlier on a trip to Jordan, and I was looking forward to continuing some of the discussions we had had at that time.

I decided to walk from the UN, since a number of streets had already been partly or fully closed due to all the high-level people who had arrived. It took me around twenty minutes. The meeting went well; Queen Noor and I had good discussions about Jordan, including what Jordan had done and what it could do more for its children and the children in its region.

Toward the end of the meeting, Queen Noor suddenly asked, "Do I really have to be at the UN at 7:20 a.m.?" This was the time she and her motorcade had been assigned. I explained the situation and informed her that if her own security people would allow her to do so, she could walk from the hotel to the UN premises and arrive at any time, as long as she arrived before nine o'clock in the morning. I told her that I had just done the walk and that it would take around twenty minutes.

"Great," she said, and then she turned to Jordan's ambassador to the UN to add, "and Mr. Ambassador, we will walk together, will we not?" The ambassador did not looked too pleased, but she walked the next day together with the ambassador. I do not know how many security people she had around her, but I am sure that they were many. When I met her at the breakfast, she thanked me and said it was an excellent idea. And the ambassador seemed to have survived.

And then the meeting was on. Looking around in the ECOSOC Chamber of the UN—seeing seventy-one heads of state or government, eighty-eight senior-level people representing their countries, forty-five NGOs, many UNICEF goodwill ambassadors, the UN secretary general, and other senior UN officials—made me aware of how this day was a cumulation of many hours of hard work by so many. I also knew it would never have happened if it had not been for Jim Grant himself, who never gave up and managed to deal with each real and imaginary obstacle. One by one, the seventy-one heads of state or government took the floor after the video and Jim Grant's brief statement. They all spoke about how to improve the situation for children in their own country and worldwide and how to have concrete goals to measure their progress. They all spoke within the allotted time of five minutes, apart from one: Prime Minister Margaret Thatcher. She gave her prepared statement of five minutes, but then she left the script and spoke for another approximately five minutes, which was actually even better than her prepared statement. The most interesting thing, however, was that the chairs, Prime Minister Mulroney of Canada and President Mussa Traore of Mali, who had given clear indications to other speakers as they approached the end of their allocated speaking time, did not dare to stop Prime Minister Thatcher.

At the end of the day, a World Declaration on the Survival, Protection, and Development of Children and a Plan of Action comprising a detailed set of child-related human development goals for year 2000 was signed.

In the early part of 1989, UN Secretary General Perez de Cuillar asked Jim Grant to lead what was going to be called Operation Lifeline Sudan in response to a devastating famine and the effects of the Sudanese Civil War. Operation Lifeline Sudan would draw from a consortium of UN agencies (mainly the World Food Programme and UNICEF) and a large number of NGOs. Its main purpose was to provide humanitarian assistance throughout Sudan's war-torn and drought-affected regions. Operation Lifeline Sudan was established in April 1989 after difficult negotiations between the UN, the Government of Sudan, and the Sudan People's Liberation Movement/Army (SPLM/A) to deliver humanitarian assistance to all civilians in need, regardless of their location or political affiliation.

In December 1990, Jim Grant asked me to go to Sudan. Among other things, he wanted me to meet with Sudan's president, Omar al-Bashir, to get his agreement that UNICEF could use a preferential exchange rate to maximize our funds' ability to assist the Sudanese people. He also wanted me to visit some of the affected areas in Sudan. Arriving in Khartoum, Sudan's capital, I was met by several people from UNICEF, the government NGOs, and the media at the airport. A middle-aged man dressed in the traditional Sudanese white outfit, *jallabiya*, approached.

He said, "I have been waiting for you." Then he gave me a very special old silver ring, saying, "I want you to have this and wear it; then no evil will happen to you." Then he left.

I am not very superstitious, but I decided to wear the ring while in Sudan. And I still have it. I tried to find out who he was; apparently, he was a well-known scholar.

The meeting with the president, who had come to power the year before during a military coup, was quite interesting. I managed to achieve what I had come for, and to make sure that he did not change his mind, I told all the journalists who were camping outside his office how grateful UNICEF and I were for the president's decision to grant us the use of the preferential exchange rate, which would benefit the people, and in particular the children, of Sudan. Maybe the ring helped!

The next day we were going south. I was sitting next to the pilot, and I was amazed that he used a regular road map for navigation, but he certainly knew what he was doing. We landed safely in El Obeid, where we had lunch with UNICEF staff members residing there. After lunch we continued to Malakal, a garrison town held at that time by the government of Sudan forces but surrounded by SPLA forces. We had negotiated safe passage for UNICEF, but so they could recognize that it was us, we had agreed that when the plane approached the airstrip for landing we would spiral down. We all hoped that this would work well, and it did.

We were going to stay in the local governor's house, which was far from a palace. UNICEF's representative in Sudan inspected the room I was going to stay in and cautiously sprayed the room and the bed with insect repellant. We had brought bottled water and soft drinks, since they were not available where we were going. While unpacking, someone discovered that the water had unfortunately been left behind, so I had a choice between brushing my teeth in Coca-Cola or tonic water. I opted for the latter.

Malakal and its population were severely affected by the drought and the civil war. We went to the health clinic for mothers and babies. I held one tiny baby in my arms whom I knew would not survive, and there was nothing I could do; it was a terrible feeling. I saw mothers in the village trying to make meals for their families, and the only thing they had was some cow skin that they boiled in water. Even though I knew that some concrete assistance was on the way, I felt so helpless not being able to do more there and then.

In November 1991, Jim Grant asked me to go to Lebanon. The NGOs of Lebanon, represented by the First Lady, had been awarded the UCI (Universal Child Immunization) Award for 1990, having achieved the goal of immunizing 80 percent of children against the six most crippling childhood diseases, a goal that had been set by the WHO and UNICEF in 1985. While it was a remarkable achievement for any country to meet this goal, it was particularly remarkable for a country like Lebanon, which had endured a variety of conflicts over more than a decade.

While the conflicts in Lebanon had more or less come to an end late 1989 and early 1990, it was not entirely without risk for a senior UN official like myself to go to Lebanon. A number of Westerners had been taken as hostages over the last several years, and while most of them now had been released, there were still some in captivity. The last American hostage had been the chief Middle East correspondent for the Associated Press when he was captured in 1985, and he was only released the day before I left New York for Lebanon. The last two known hostages held by Lebanese militants were still in captivity, two German aid workers. They were released the following year, in June 1992. When Jim Grant asked me to go, he stressed that both my gender and nationality would make it less risky for me than others. It would have been out of the question for an American to go at the time.

Back then, one could not secure tickets for any flights to Lebanon from the United States. I was booked on a flight to Paris and then given tickets for Middle East Airlines. Upon arrival in Paris, I would have to go to the ticket counter, where my tickets to and from Damascus from Paris would be exchanged for similar tickets to and from Beirut. I was already booked on the flights. On arrival in Paris, I followed the instructions given to me, and they worked well.

I was met with a lot of security on arrival in Beirut. Apart from a few military officers for the UNIFIL (United Nations Interim Force in Lebanon), I was apparently the only guest at the hotel. I was told that in addition to the hotel security, a UNICEF security person would be stationed outside the door to my room every night.

While one could see signs of Beirut normalizing, it was a terrible sight, with many buildings bombed and damaged. Of course, in addition to all the physical damage, the psychological damage was enormous. As always, it had had a major impact on children. UNICEF had continued over many years to assist NGOs, and more and more, as a direct part of programs, to arrange summer camps for children. These peace camps were a way to get children from across ethnic and religious backgrounds to meet each other to share human and social values through creative and recreational activities.

The award ceremony, which was held on December 9, went well. In my speech, I stressed the ethical foundation of the World Summit for Children that children's essential needs should be given a first call on society's resources in bad as well as in good times, in times of war as well as in times of peace.

The days before and after the ceremony, I traveled, with two security guards and other UNICEF staff, across the entire country—from east to west and from north to south—to meet with NGOs and with children.

The UNIFIL had its headquarters and main operations in Southern Lebanon. My brother Hans, who is a police officer and who trained in special forces and worked in the Norwegian Police Counterterrorism Unit, had decided to volunteer to serve in the UNIFIL when it was established in 1978. Norway contributed a sizable number of troops to the UNIFIL, so I knew about its operations from his year in service with them.

The UNIFIL had worked very well with UNICEF in a number of areas and had in particular assisted with rehabilitating children who had lost limbs from land mines, so it seemed important for me to visit their headquarters. A UNIFIL helicopter picked us up in Beirut early in the morning and arrived at the UNIFIL headquarters in the outskirts of the town of Naqoura, which borders Israel, where it had been since it was established in 1978. There I got a big surprise. A major from the UNIFIL force had been assigned to accompany me during my visit, and it turned out to be someone who was in my class in high school. I had met him a number of times during our high-school reunions, and I knew he worked for the Ministry of Foreign Affairs in Oslo. He told me that he had taken a leave-of-absence to join the UNIFIL and that when he heard I was coming, he volunteered to accompany me during my visit, which I greatly appreciated. I spent an interesting day with the UNIFIL, and I also met some local families whose children had had limbs amputated after land-mine explosions where they were playing. The UNIFIL forces had as much as possible tried to assist in clearing areas of unexploded anti-personnel land mines, and they also assisted the families by providing wheelchairs, prostheses, and other medical help. UNICEF continued to work on trauma counseling, both for the affected children and their families.

Back in Beirut, during my last day before leaving Lebanon, the staff had arranged for a get-together with wonderful Lebanese food and music. The staff members had been fantastic; they worked throughout the years of conflict, all of them Lebanese (apart from the representative) and affected by the conflict themselves but never giving up on trying to make life better for all children in Lebanon.

After a short stay in New York, I was off to Liberia, another country affected by conflicts. The First Liberian Civil War had started in 1989 and would last until 1997. Unfortunately, there would be more civil wars after that. There were no regular flights to Liberia, so I first went to Abidjan, Cote d'Ivoire, and continued the next day to Monrovia, the capital of Liberia. The UNICEF regional director for West and Central Africa was going to join me, and the UNICEF representative in Liberia was also in Abidjan and would return to Monrovia with us. The flying time between Abidjan and Monrovia was around one and a half hours by a charter flight that could carry both some cargo and passengers. Not only did they weigh our luggage, including hand luggage, but they also needed the passengers' weights, which I did not find too reassuring. The flight went fine, without any problems. The UNICEF representative had stocked some things for us, including croissants that we would get for breakfast the next few days.

Liberia was divided in a few zones, each occupied by a different faction with different self-proclaimed governments. Amos Sawyer was the interim president in the Interim Government of National Unity covering Monrovia and its surrounding environments, and Charles Taylor's National Patriotic Front of Liberia, with its headquarters in Gbarnga, was northeast of Monrovia. UNICEF, as it had done since its establishment in 1946, worked on all sides of the conflicts, focusing on children.

One of the many challenges in Liberia was the recruitment and use of child soldiers. It is estimated that as many as fifteen thousand children served as soldiers during the civil wars, and all factions used child soldiers.

Unfortunately, it was not difficult to recruit child soldiers, some of them as young as twelve years old. Many of them had seen their villages or homes destroyed, seen family members tortured and killed, and were easily convinced that joining as soldiers could enable them to get revenge and/or could ensure the safety of the rest of their families. Adequate food would also easily attract children who had not had enough food for long periods. UNICEF was trying as much as possible to support the demobilization of child soldiers and the universality of adequate education.

Charles Taylor and his National Patriotic Front had set up a sort of government at the headquarters in Gbarnga, with ministers in a number of areas, including health and education. It had been negotiated in advance that I would join in a visit to Gbarnga, and we had been promised free passage. Charles Taylor had written a letter to UNICEF stating this, which was copied and taped to the windscreens of the three vehicles we were going to use.

The drive from Monrovia to Gbarnga would normally take around two to three hours, but with all the checkpoints, we knew it would take much longer. All the vehicles were equipped with radios, and we would regularly check in with the office in Monrovia, but every time we were close to a checkpoint we needed radio silence.

At almost all checkpoints were child soldiers, most of them with assault rifles, such as AK-47s or M-16s. Most people may not be aware, but these weapons are relatively simple to use. The AK-47 can easily be stripped and reassembled by a twelve-year-old child.

At every checkpoint we were stopped, and we could see that most of the child soldiers were more or less intoxicated from alcohol or drugs or both. They always ordered us out of the cars and did not pay attention or did not understand when we explained that Charles Taylor himself had guaranteed us free passage, showing them the letter taped on the windscreen. They checked the vehicles, some of them pointing their guns at us while others did a search. None of us could be sure whether they would pull the trigger or not at any given moment.

After almost five hours of driving, we safely reached Gbarnga. It turned out that Charles Taylor was not present, unfortunately; we had really hoped to meet with him. However, we met with a number of other people responsible for health, education, water, and sanitation, which were all areas where UNICEF was giving support.

We expressed strong concerns about what we had seen on our way to Gbarnga in terms of child soldiers, particularly the number of child soldiers under the age of fifteen. UNICEF was trying to assist with demobilizing the child soldiers, starting with the youngest ones first. Our goal was to make sure they all go to school, along with many other goals connected to their wellness and safety. After a late lunch, we headed back to Monrovia. The checkpoints went slightly easier, and we did not see as many child soldiers at them. We suspected that people from Gbarnga had been "cleaning up" and giving orders before we left. On our way to Monrovia, we managed to lose our radio contact with the office. There was not much we could do; we tried to reconnect many times. The staff in the office apparently got into a panic. They were asking themselves, "What are we going to do and say if they call from New York? We cannot really say that we have lost radio contact with the deputy executive director and the people accompanying her."

Just after we went through the last checkpoint, there were three UNICEF vehicles waiting for us, and they were extremely happy to see that we were all okay.

Jim Grant continued traveling all over the world to do as much as he could for the world's children. He was seventy-two and did not show any signs of slowing down. But then he suddenly did not look like his usual self, and we learned that he had pancreatic cancer. He had surgery, radiation, and chemo, and again he refused to slow down. He felt that he had so much more to do. We all hoped that he would be okay, but after a while we could see that he did not look well again. Nevertheless, he rarely mentioned his illness and continued to travel to meet with prime ministers and presidents. Even when he had to stop traveling, he did not stop working. We, the senior staff, went to his residence in Croton and worked with him from there. He even had some IT staff come to teach him to use the computer, something he had had no time to learn until then. He received letters of well wishes from around the world, from presidents and prime ministers. And he wrote letters challenging many of them to do better for children in their countries. One of the last letters he wrote was to President Bill Clinton, urging him to sign and ratify the Convention on the Rights of the Child, which the United States had not done.

The last few days of his life he spent in the hospital. I had a bad cold and did not want to go for fear of spreading it in the hospital. The last day of his life, drifting in and out of consciousness, he decided, from what I was told by one of his sons, to call a few people, including me, to say goodbye. When I got the call, one of Jim Grant's sons put him on. He thanked me for all I had done for UNICEF and the children of the world. A few hours later, he was gone. The memory of his last phone call—and even more, the memory of this extraordinary man—will stay with me forever.

The memorial service for Jim Grant took place in St. John the Divine Cathedral in New York on February 10, 1995, with more than 2,500 people present. First Lady Hillary Clinton, representing President Bill Clinton, attended to honor Jim Grant. In her speech, she said that President Clinton had instructed Secretary of State Warren Christopher to take the necessary steps so that United States would sign the Convention on the Rights of the Child, and she added that Madeleine Albright, the US's permanent representative to the United Nations, would do so within a week. She also said, "Nobody fought harder for this convention and its noble cause than Jim Grant. That was one of the last things he was in communication with the president about before his death."

I was present when Ambassador Albright signed the convention on behalf of the United States a week or so later. Unfortunately, the United States has still not ratified the Convention on the Rights of the Child.

7

Stanley

I met Stanley for the first time in January 1987. I was the acting deputy executive director for UNICEF, a position I would hold for most of that year, until I was officially appointed to the position in December. Stanley was an account executive for SAS, Scandinavian Airlines, whose client responsibility included all parts of the United Nations. He had just had a meeting with the UNICEF Travel Section, one of the many areas under my oversight, and they had apparently suggested that he should meet with me.

What do I remember of this first meeting? Apart from our discussions about my and UNICEF staff members' travel to and from Scandinavia, I remember a well-dressed and quite good-looking man with a dark gray suit and a firm handshake. I also remember noting that he had a memorable last name.

Over the next couple of years, Stanley called from time to time to follow up on my travels and to check whether everything was working to UNICEF's satisfaction. He came to visit me once more in 1988 after we had moved into the new UNICEF House on Forty-Fourth Street between First and Second Avenues and I had become the deputy executive director.

In December 1988, Stanley called me to ask whether I was available to join him as Scandinavian Airlines' guest at a pre-Christmas luncheon hosted by the Norwegian-American Chamber of Commerce. I was aware of the event but had originally decided not to go since I was extremely busy; however, when Stanley asked me in his very nice voice, it sounded tempting. I decided to accept the invitation. The luncheon was held at a hotel less than ten minutes' walking distance from my office, which made it convenient as well. We were sitting next to each other at a table with around ten people, but after a while it was as if none of the others existed. We talked about our families and ourselves, and we discovered that we had at least one thing in common: we were both family-oriented. Stanley knew that I would be traveling shortly thereafter, and at some stage he suggested that we should talk further when I was back. Then he asked whether I wanted him to pick me up at the airport upon my return on New Year's Day. I don't know what made me say yes; I actually said, "That would be very nice." After the luncheon, Stanley, as a perfect gentleman, walked me back to my office. He told me later that he had wanted to kiss me but did not dare—which was most likely wise of him.

During my stay in Stockholm and Oslo, I thought about Stanley a few times. I had actually brought his business card, thinking that I might call him and tell him not to pick me up on my return. But I did not do that. I actually thought he might have forgotten the whole thing by then.

On New Year's Day I returned to New York. As always, my office had arranged for a UNICEF driver to pick me up at the airport.

It was a cold afternoon when I arrived in New York, and I was happy I had my fur coat on. I picked up my suitcase and proceeded through customs, which went smoothly, and exited to the arrival hall. There I saw Stanley in the corner of my eye—with a bouquet of red roses—and a UNICEF driver in the other corner. I knew I had to make a fast decision, so when the driver, who had already seen me, came forward to help me with my suitcase, and Stanley also came forward, I said to the driver, who luckily was not the regular driver, "I am so sorry that you were not told that Mr. Sham Poo is picking me up and that you had to come all the way to the airport on a New Year's Day."

He said that it was no problem at all but also told me that he had some papers for me as well as a case of wine that somebody had given me. I told him that we should transfer that to Stanley's car, which we did. Stanley had by then already wished me Happy New Year and given me the beautiful red roses. (He told me some time later how difficult it had been to find a place selling nice roses on New Year's Day.) His car was a big blue Cadillac Seville, and it was very comfortable. After I was seated in the car, Stanley asked whether I would like a glass of champagne to start the new year.

I said yes, thinking we would stop somewhere for that. However, while still at the airport's parking, Stanley went out, opened the trunk of the car, and came back with two beautiful crystal goblets, each with a nice white napkin tied around the stem, and a bottle of champagne, which he opened. We drank a glass each and again wished each other Happy New Year. What a way to start a new year!

After having given Stanley my address, I told him that I had an engagement a few hours later. I'd been invited to a New Year's Day party that my colleague and good friend Mike Shower had every year, and I told Stanley that I would be overjoyed if he could join me. When Stanley parked his car, the doorman was already out to help with my luggage and case of wine, which he helped bring to my apartment on the twenty-ninth floor. I asked Stanley to make himself comfortable and have a drink while I was took a shower and changed. Mike Shower lived on West Ninth. Street in Greenwich Village. We took a taxi, which was easier than driving in Stanley's car and trying to find a place to park.

I had been to Mike's apartment on many occasions, but this was the first time I had ever brought a friend. A number of people were there already when we arrived, including people working for UNICEF or the US Committee for UNICEF and related organizations, as well as some friends of Mike. Since I had been away for a couple of weeks, many people wanted to talk to me. I was a little concerned that Stanley would feel left out, but I could see that he handled it all well and was talking with people he had never met before, which impressed me.

New Year's Day 1989 was on a Sunday, so the next day was also a work holiday. Stanley and I had breakfast at a diner close to my apartment, and we continued our conversations from the day before. We already knew a little about each other, but now I learned that he had been married once many years before and had one eighteen-year-old-daughter named Yuen and a twenty-six-year-old stepdaughter named Lisa. I also learned that he had lost a brother, Chong, suddenly from a brain aneurism just a little over a year before, that they had been very close, and that they had shared the apartment where he lived. After that, we started seeing each other regularly, particularly on weekends when I was not traveling.

Even though I had not planned to develop a more permanent relationship with any man, it started to happen. I had warned Stanley that it would not be easy to be with me. Apart from my frequent travels, the fact that I was a high-ranking woman in the UN system meant that my private life was not that private; people would start to scrutinize him as well if he was seen with me regularly. Stanley did not seem too worried. I soon realized that Stanley could deal with anybody, whether a prime minister or a garbage collector, in the same comfortable way. Another important strength of his was that he did not seem threatened or intimidated by being with a woman who had a much higher position in society than he did—something rare among men in our generation and even among younger men today.

Stanley had one brother and a number of cousins living in New York, and he brought me to meet all of them. They were all used to him having a long string of girlfriends over the years, so in the beginning they seemed to think this was just another short-lived relationship, but after a while they all realized that this was different.

Stanley also brought me to meet his long-term friend and colleague Kathleen, also called KC, and her mother. KC and I liked each other from the start, and we have continued to be close friends and see each other often.

While I did not have any family in New York, my dear friends John and Mehr came closest. I told them about Stanley, and they invited us for dinner. While it did not show, Stanley told me later that he'd been very nervous. He'd felt it was an important test that he could not afford to fail. He certainly passed, and Mehr and John continue to be special friends to both of us.

A few months later, Stanley asked me to marry him. While I really loved him, I was not yet prepared to make such a commitment. I told him I had to think about it. While many men would not have taken this well, Stanley did. He waited patiently. After a few months, he tried again. We had attended a reception hosted by Eve Labouisse, the wife of the second executive director of UNICEF, Henry Labouisse. I had met them both a year or so before he passed away. She took a liking toward me, and we met from time to time. She was an interesting person with even more interesting parents, Marie and Henri Curie. When she invited me to this reception, I asked whether it was okay to bring a friend, to which she responded very positively. She greeted Stanley with a big smile. After the reception, which was held in her beautiful Sutton Place apartment, Stanley and I went into the garden on the ground floor. And there, surrounded by flowers and trees, Stanley asked me again to marry him, and this time I said yes. He took a gold ring from his pinky finger, a ring that his mother had given him many years earlier, and placed it on my ring finger.

Now we started to plan our life together, and it was exciting. We went on a brief trip to Oslo so Stanley could meet my parents, my two brothers, my sister-in-law, my daughter and her husband, and my wonderful granddaughter, Sonja, who had just turned one year. They all liked Stanley from the time they met him. My father in particular, with whom I had always been very close, was well pleased to see me so happy.

Upon returning to New York, we started to look for a place to live. Before dating Stanley, I had already started to look for an apartment outside the city. It had been nice to live in Manhattan for a few years, as I had gotten to know the city well, but I had decided that the time had come to buy something—and since I was alone at the time, I thought an apartment would be the best. Now the plans had changed. We wanted to buy a house. Meanwhile, my daughter and her family had decided to come to New York, and they wanted to know if we would be willing to house them, at least for a while. I had to discuss this with Stanley, and he said yes at once. We decided to look for a house big enough to house all of us.

I got the name of a real estate agent from a colleague in UNICEF. We met and put together some criteria for houses we would be interested in looking at. When you are two busy people like Stanley and me, it is not easy to schedule time to look at houses. Sometimes we looked at a house together; sometimes only one of us went. In total, we looked at more than twenty-five houses. One day, Stanley looked at a house in Scarsdale, which is in Westchester County, New York. He liked it and suggested I look at it too. I did, and I liked it. Then we went to see the house again together. We decided this was it: we would put in a bid slightly lower than the asking price. The real estate agent came back with a positive response—the house was ours. After going through all the formalities, we bought the house, and on September 1, 1989, we all moved in. Stanley and I continue to live in this house, which is now more than one hundred years old, and we continue to be very happy there. Neither of us have ever lived in one place this long before.

I had already introduced Stanley to Jim Grant and some of my other colleagues, and when it was possible for him to do so, taking into account the type of job he had, he would start to accompany me to important receptions and other functions. Stanley is a people person. What is, as I've said, particularly striking about him is that he interacts as easily with the queen of Spain as he does with our mailman in Scarsdale, and he loves to interact with people.

While I had met Stanley's family in New York, it was eventually time to go to Trinidad and Tobago to meet the rest of his family, especially his mother. I discuss this at length in the chapter called "Trinidad and Tobago."

While we had already made a big commitment by buying a house together, we were still not formally married. We had no plans to have a big wedding; we were thinking we'd have something simple down at the city hall. We also had to find the right time in between my travels and Stanley's work schedule. So, we went to get our marriage license as the first step. We had already asked our good friends KC and Mehr to be our witnesses, which they were happy to be. When we waited in line to get our license, we also saw couples waiting in line to get married. Stanley then said that it would be nice to get married in a church instead, and he suggested I could maybe ask the pastor in the Norwegian Seamen's Church whether he would be willing to marry us. In the Norwegian Church, it is up to the individual pastor (or at least it was at that time) whether he or she was willing to marry a divorced couple. I had already been on the board of the church for three years, knew the pastor well, and felt fairly confident that he would say yes. So I gave him a call, and he said of course he would be willing; he asked what date we had in mind. I said May 9, since I was traveling a few days after that. Unfortunately, it turned out that he would be in Washington that day, but if we really wanted him to do it and not the other pastor, he suggested Sunday, May 10, after the regular service. That was no problem for us. It turned out that that Sunday was also Mother's Day. We got married in the church with a touching sermon, and Mehr and KC were our witnesses. The other people present were Mehr's husband, John; KC's mother and her sister, Carole; KC's two sons; Stanley's brother, Orlan, and his wife; UNICEF's executive director, Jim Grant, and his wife and their dog; and a few other UNICEF colleagues. Mehr and John had generously offered to host a small reception for us in their apartment afterward, which was extremely nice. And later that evening, Stanley and I went out for dinner with his brother and his wife.

At the end of the annual UNICEF Executive Board meeting, I had for a few years invited people to my apartment in Manhattan for a get-together. Having always worked long hours, especially during our board meetings, I served relatively simple fare. I ordered some Norwegian specialties from a store in Brooklyn and made some salads. I had told Stanley about this, and some time before the board meeting, Stanley asked me whether I wanted him to help. He said he would be happy to cook some food. I already knew that Stanley's cooking was excellent, so I was delighted to accept. Very few people knew him at that time, so I could see that others wondered who this man was who seemed to know his way around my apartment. But they all enjoyed the food very much. After we moved to Scarsdale, Stanley was happy to serve a larger-scale meal for a bigger crowd. For the first few years, the board meeting was still in April, so it was a little risky to invite sixty to seventy people, given the unpredictable weather. But we were always lucky. Apart from a little drizzle from time to time, the weather was always nice. When the annual board meeting was moved to June, it was easier. We had, however, bought a large, very nice tent, which we set up in the garden. Stanley had also bought some professional chafing dishes. He cooked all the food himself. I was allowed to chop some ingredients, and sometimes KC was too, but Stanley did the rest. We became more and more experienced with knowing what to serve, and how to set the whole thing up. The food and drinks were all served on real china plates and in glasses; we had enough plates and glasses for more than one hundred guests. Stanley would try out new dishes on me leading up to the event. The guests loved both the food and the atmosphere.

Like many people from Trinidad and Tobago, Stanley is of mixed heritage. His mother was French, Creole, African, and Chinese, and his father was Chinese. Stanley's father, "Apo" Sham Shie Poo, was born in RenHe Town in the Baiyun District in Guanzhou around 1900. He immigrated to Trinidad in the late 1930s. The Chinese were a relatively small but important part of the population that had been migrating to Trinidad since 1806. Trinidad, being a British colony at that time, normally gave the immigrants an English name, and Stanley's father became Desmond Sham Poo. He was a very good cook and soon became the head chef at Shantung Restaurant on Queen Street in Port of Spain. Like so many other Chinese who arrived at that time, he had left a wife and a son back in China. In Trinidad, he met Stanley's mother, Yvonne, and started a common-law relationship with her. They had three sons— Stanley, Anthony (who, as I mentioned earlier, suddenly died in 1987), and Desmond. In addition to their regular English names, they all got Chinese names—Stanley Simming, Anthony Simchong, and Desmond Simlon. Stanley's family here and in Trinidad as well as some of his childhood friends still mostly address him using his Chinese name.

When Stanley was around nine years old, his parents split up. His father moved from Port of Spain and set up a grocery shop where he also had a license to serve liquor and some food (often called a "rum shop" in Trinidad at the time); the shop was in Penal, in south Trinidad, south of the second-largest city, San Fernando. When Stanley was sixteen, his father got sick, so Stanley left school to help in the store and, under his father's supervision, do the cooking. His father gradually improved and recovered. Stanley also assisted his father in transforming the shop to a mini mart, which was very successful.

In 1961, Stanley's father sent for his wife from China, and the following year, their son San Chuen, who was thirty-three, arrived. Stanley and his brothers called the wife "Ma" and the brother "Tai Ko," which means "big brother."

After the Black Power uprising in Trinidad in 1970, Stanley's father did the same as a number of other Chinese and left the country. Stanley had already immigrated to the United States two years earlier, but his father did not see the United States as a country where he could establish a business easily, so he decided, together with his son and wife, to return to China. In addition to a business that he established in Guangzhou, he also had a business in Macau.

One summer night in 1975, Stanley had a nightmare about his father, and when he woke up, he had the feeling that his father had died. Two weeks later, he got a letter from his mother in Trinidad informing him that his father had died in China the same night that he had had the nightmare.

From discussions Stanley and I had about his father, I could strongly feel that Stanley had had a lack of closure with him. While he knew that his father died in Guangzhou, China, he did not know exactly where. He did not know whether his stepmother was still alive or where his brother San Chuen was. He had heard from some relatives that they thought he was somewhere in Canada, but they were not sure.

In 1992, I went to conference on child health in Guangzhou for a few days. I was sorry that Stanley had not joined me so that he could be near the area where his father was born, had spent many years of his life, and died. An even better opportunity emerged, however, the following year. Jim Grant, who already had started his health battle, asked me to attend a major international conference on mother and child health in Beijing, China. The director general of the WHO (World Health Organization) and I, on behalf of UNICEF, would be the two main speakers at the opening of the conference. Jim Grant also suggested that the UNICEF office plan a few weeks traveling in China to visit the poorest provinces where the main UNICEF-supported activities took place. This was a unique opportunity, and I had to make sure Stanley joined me.

Stanley was excited, so we started to discuss how to get more information on exactly where his father was from. Maybe he even had some relatives in China. Stanley had an idea to get more information: he had three cousins who had migrated from Trinidad to Toronto, Canada, many years before. The oldest of these cousins was born in China. When Stanley called his cousin, he got excited and told Stanley that his daughter was getting married in a couple of weeks. He asked if we could come and also said he would see what he could do to assist with information. So off we went to Toronto for just a little more than a twenty-four-hour visit. The wedding was a big affair, with around 250 guests and a lot of fantastic Chinese food. The cousin, who could still speak and write Chinese, wrote a "To whom it may concern" letter in Chinese characters that said, "This is the son of Sham Shie Poo from RenHe Town in Baiyun District in Guangzhou; I am looking for my ancestral village." As soon as we were back in New York, I faxed this letter to UNICEF in Beijing. They sent it to one of their major counterparts, All China Women's Federation, one of the largest NGOs in the world—it had more than sixty thousand offices throughout China.

We were on our way to China, and Bejing was our first stop.

The next two and a half weeks would be hectic between visiting

UNICEF-supported activities in some of the poorest provinces, meeting with counterpart ministries, visiting cultural cites, and attending daily official lunches and dinners with the most exquisite Chinese food one could imagine. We had interpreters with us throughout the trip, one of them a bright woman named Hongwey whose English was perfect. She worked in MOFTEC (Ministry of Foreign Trade and External Cooperation). She had been part of the Chinese delegation to the UNICEF Executive Board Meeting a couple of times, so I had met her before. With some support from my side, Hongwey later joined UNICEF and advanced to be UNICEF representative to a number of countries. She is still with UNICEF as a representative, and we are still in touch from time to time. UNICEF's deputy representative to China also accompanied us throughout the trip. The deputy representative was married to the Norwegian journalist who had been UNICEF's deputy director of information when I joined the organization.

After one week of traveling, we were going to Guangzhou. It was only in the minibus taking us to the airport to fly to Guangzhou that we were told that they had been able to locate Stanley's father's family and the grave were he was buried. It was hard to stay calm after that. Arriving in Guangzhou, we were met by officials and media and taken by police escort to a beautiful new mansion that stood alone, as there were no other houses nearby. (We have seen pictures in recent years showing that the area is now much more developed, with many new houses around.) Outside the house was a large group of people, and we were told they were all family. I was skeptical, but then I looked at some of them: they had exactly the same distinct eyebrows as Stanley, and one of them looked a lot like his cousin in Toronto, who was born in China. I told Stanley, "This is real." The woman who was the interpreter at this leg of the trip told us that the house belonged to his brother San Chuen, who many years earlier had migrated to Vancouver with his family, including his mother, who was still alive. He had been back regularly to, among other things, build this nice, modern house. The Chinese authorities keep good track of what they call "overseas Chinese," and when they started to find Stanley's family, they had called San Chuen in Vancouver to ask whether he had a brother named Stanley "Simming" Sham Poo. He confirmed that that was correct, and when he was told that Stanley was on his way to China, he asked that he be given his phone number in Vancouver so they could talk on the phone upon his return to New York. All the people outside were related to Stanley, and all of it was very emotional.

After some speeches by government officials, Stanley and I were taken with some refreshments through the narrow streets to Stanley's father's old house. One of the old relatives lived there and took care of the house. And there we experienced another emotional surprise: on the wall were old pictures of relatives, including pictures of Stanley and his two brothers when they were kids. There were also a couple of old pictures of Stanley's father when he was young, and a young relative who could speak a little English volunteered to have the pictures copied so we could bring them back with us to New York. We had them framed, and they now hang on our picture wall in our New York home. There was also a shrine for Stanley's father in the house. We prayed and lit incense, which was again so emotional. Throughout the whole trip, government officials videotaped every important event, including this, and when we watch it again so many years later, tears still come to our eyes. The final important act of closure for Stanley was to go to his father's grave. Again we prayed and lit incense. The journey had given Stanley the closure he needed and had prayed for, and I felt so fortunate and happy to be a part of it.

Back in New York a few weeks later, another emotional stage began: Stanley called his brother in Vancouver. They had not talked in more than twenty years. His English had certainly not improved since they'd seen each other in Trinidad, but they had no problems understanding each other. He wanted us to come visit, and we decided that we could take a couple of days off to do so around Thanksgiving.

The few days we spent in Vancouver were extraordinary. Chinese people do not always easily express their feelings in public. But the emotions expressed by Stanley and his brother when they hugged each other at the airport showed that they were not afraid of displaying their feelings. Arriving at their house, we met Ma, who was so excited to see Stanley. She did not speak any English, and she was in her nineties, with poor hearing, but that did not matter. The communication was there. Later we met Tai Ko's three sons (two of them chefs at big restaurants as their grandfather had been), their wives, and their children. Tai Ko's oldest granddaughter, Eva, a nurse, who was born in China, was the perfect interpreter when needed. Every day they took us to a different Chinese restaurant, including the two where the sons where chefs. We were served the best Chinese food one could imagine, and we felt as if we were back in China.

We continued to be in touch with Stanley's family in Vancouver. The following year, Stanley's brother Desmond visited us from Trinidad, and we all went to Vancouver. Tai Ko, his wife, and their granddaughter, Eva, also visited us in New York, and a few years later we went to Vancouver for Eva's wedding, an extraordinary Chinese event. Tai Ko had had health problems since his mid-sixties, but it was his wife who unfortunately suddenly passed away after a stroke. We saw him once more when we went to Vancouver for one of the grandnephews' weddings. We could see he was diminished by multiple health issues but still overjoyed to see us. He passed away two years later, when we were on our way to Trinidad; it became too complicated for us to go to the funeral, which was going to take place just a couple of days later. Stanley and I are so happy to have all the memories, which we cherish so much. This was another important chapter in our lives.

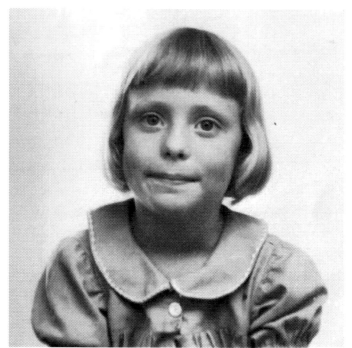

Me, 1948

Me, graduation from high school 1962

Thomas, my father

Ruth, my mother

Stanley and his mother Yvonne, 1968

Stanley and me, our wedding day, May 10, 1992

My first carnival 1990

My mother's 90th birthday. Me, Elizabeth, Sonja and my mother Ruth

Stanley and me
Carnival 2012

Stanley and me 2017

8

Trinidad and Tobago

I arrived in Trinidad in November 1989 and fell immediately in love with the country and its people.

A number of Stanley's family members, including his mother, Yvonne, were at the airport to meet us. Stanley told me that that had never happened before. I received such a warm welcome.

We were coming from a cool and rainy November in New York, and stepping out from the airport, the warm tropical air met us. It was late night, and it felt very comfortable.

Driving from the airport to Stanley's mother's house was a little over an hour drive. I pleasantly remember all the lights on the hills we passed.

Stanley's mother had a big house where her youngest daughter, Denise, and Denise's three-year-old daughter, Raynese, stayed on weekends. When Stanley's mother had expanded the house a few years earlier, she'd wanted to make sure it had enough bedrooms to accommodate any of her children when they were visiting., so Stanley had his own bedroom always ready for him whenever he visited.

Our visit coincided with Stanley's mother's sixty-ninth birthday. Over all the years since Stanley had left Trinidad in 1968, he had always made sure that he returned home on or close to his mother's birthday. Stanley was his mother's favorite. When some of the younger siblings still lived at home, they would say, "The prince is coming," when Stanley came visiting. And he always brought a lot of food that may be difficult or expensive to get in Trinidad or other things that he felt his mother might need. He also brought things for his younger siblings. Stanley has always been a person who cares for others.

Stanley's mother was a remarkable woman. She had brought up eight children very well, and she had always worked hard. We got along well. One day she told me that I was the angel she had been waiting for to take care of her son; she was so happy that he had found somebody like me.

Among other things, we had brought a big turkey for her birthday. I am sure Stanley cooked as well, since I remember we had a lot of food, but the only thing I remember clearly was how my mother-in-law made the turkey and the stuffing. For the stuffing she made a mix of chicken liver, bread stuffing, and herbs. After she had baked the turkey and the stuffing, she cooled it off a little bit and then sliced the turkey in nice slices, filled each slice with some stuffing, and closed each with a toothpick. It tasted and looked fantastic. While I learned how to make the stuffing from her, I have never managed the way she rolled the slices with the stuffing within.

One morning I was watching my mother-in-law make another interesting and new-to-me dish called *buljol*. I understand there are a few varieties, but I love her version. I watched carefully so I could replicate it later. You use salted fish, preferably boneless and skinless cod, soak it in boiling water for thirty to forty minutes, squeeze as much water as possible from the cod using paper towel, and then shred it finely. The shredded cod is then mixed with chopped onion, chopped tomatoes, and a little chopped hot pepper, lime or lemon juice, and olive oil. Once it's well mixed, you chill it in the fridge. Stanley was pleasantly surprised the first time I made it for him in New York. I learned also that *buljol* comes from French and is a combination of the words *brûlée*, which means burnt, and *gueule*, which means muzzle; in Patois the term was changed into *bu'n jaw*, which finally became *buljol*. The name does not reflect the temperature of the dish, since it is served cold, but the hotness of the hot pepper.

Both family and friends came by for my mother-in-law's birthday. I had briefly met some of them, but now I met the entire family in Trinidad. Stanley had two brothers, Simlon and Everal, and three sisters, Emily, Jennie, and Denise, who lived in Trinidad at that time with children. Then he had two nephews, Alberto and Jesus, who were the sons of his late brother Chung (or Simchung) and their mother, Lydia, who had two additional children. Almost everybody came, and they all enjoyed the food.

Stanley still had many friends in Trinidad, some of them from childhood and some from his youth. Some special friends were the Thomas family from Oxford Street in Port of Spain. They were a big family. Mama and Daddy Thomas, which Stanley called them and I started to do as well, were both still alive at that time. They had nine children, seven of them in Trinidad; one other was in Canada and another in England. Two of the Thomas women, Bella and Shirley, also came by for my mother-in-law's birthday, and we were all happy to meet each other, since they had heard about me and I had heard about them. Our friendship with the entire Thomas family has continued all of these years. Mama and Daddy Thomas are now gone, and unfortunately, in September 2016, Shirley passed away after fighting cancer for quite a while.

Trinidad and Tobago is a country with a fascinating history and an interesting mix of people. I have always loved history, and I am of the opinion that unless you know a country's history, you will not be able to understand its present. Since I did not know much about Trinidad and Tobago, I started soon after my first visit to read books, both fiction and non-fiction, about the country. The population now is around 1.4 million. The majority lives in Trinidad, which is the largest of the two islands; only around fifty thousand live in Tobago. The island of Trinidad was a Spanish colony from the arrival of Christopher Columbus in 1498 to the eventual capitulation of the Spanish Governor Don Jose Maria Chacon upon the arrival of a British fleet of eighteen warships on February 18, 1797. During the same period, the island of Tobago changed hands among Spanish, French, and Dutch colonizers, more times than any other island in the Caribbean. Trinidad and Tobago were separate until 1889. The country of Trinidad and Tobago obtained independence in 1962 and became a republic in 1976. The 2011 census showed the following ethnic mix in the population: 36 percent were of Indian descent (in Trinidad and Tobago this group is called East-Indian), 34 percent were of African descent, 23 percent were mixed, and 7 percent were small groups of people of Chinese, European, indigenous, and Syrian/Lebanese descent.

While Trinidad was never a French colony, the French have had an important impact on the country and its history. There were only a limited number of people from Spain who populated Trinidad, and in 1776, the Spanish king issued what was called a *Cedula de Poblacion* that granted free land and tax exemption for ten years to foreign settlers of the Roman Catholic faith who were willing to swear allegiance to the King of Spain. The land grant was thirty-two acres for each free man, woman, and child, and half of that for each slave that they brought to the country. A number of French nationals took advantage of this, which increased during the French Revolution. French planters and their slaves and free colored people from the neighboring islands of Martinique, Saint Lucia, Grenada, Guadeloupe, and Dominica migrated to Trinidad, and the population increased from just under fourteen hundred people in 1776 to fifteen thousand by the end of 1789. And when Trinidad became a British colony in 1797, the population had increased to eighteen thousand. It became a British colony with a French-speaking population and with Spanish laws. British rule led to an influx of settlers from the United Kingdom and the British colonies in the eastern Caribbean.

After slavery was abolished, plantation owners were in severe need of labor. The British authorities filled this need by instituting a system of indentureship, mostly from India. This started in 1845 and lasted until 1917, during which time more than 147,000 Indians were brought to Trinidad. The formerly indentured people came to constitute a vital and significant part of the population, as did the ex-slaves.

Trinidad and Tobago is also diverse when it comes to religion. According to the 2011 census, 22 percent at the time were Roman Catholics, 18 percent were Hindus, 12 percent were Pentecostal/evangelical Christians, and 5 percent were Muslims. The remaining population is made of Spiritual Shouter Baptists, other Baptists, Anglicans, Presbytarians, Methodists, Jehovah's Witnesses, Seventh-Day-Adventists, Trinidad Orisha, and Rastafarians. There is also a small Jewish community and a small Buddhist community in the country. What has always impressed me is that the population of Trinidad and Tobago is very tolerant of other people's religions, and many celebrate other religious holidays than their own.

While we were in Trinidad, we were planning our next trip for February 1990 to coincide with Carnival. While I had briefly experienced Carnival when I visited Bolivia in 1986, I wanted to know as much as possible about

Carnival in Trinidad. The Carnival tradition, or Mas (for masquerades) as they call it in Trinidad, started in the late eighteenth century with the French plantation owners organizing masquerades and balls before starting the fasting of Lent. These had been tradition in France and Italy and many other Catholic European countries. The slaves were not allowed to take part in Carnival, and they formed their own parallel celebration called Canboulay (from the French *cannes brûlée*, meaning burnt cane). These two types of celebrations have not just influenced the Trinidad Carnival of today but also the development of music in Trinidad and Tobago.

While some of the activities leading up to Carnival start just after Christmas, the main activities start just before Carnival itself. The Carnival parade of the bands takes place every year on the Monday and Tuesday before Ash Wednesday, which is the start of Lent and the period of not eating any meat. While some Catholics still follow this, not all do.

When you participate in Carnival in Trinidad, one calls it "playing Mas." There are a large number of carnival bands of various sizes. Each band has a number of sections, and each section has the same theme of costume.

Another main Carnival event is Panorama, which is held the Saturday before Carnival at the Queen's Park Savannah in Port of Spain. The Panorama competition is a significant feature of Trinidad and Tobago's Carnival and is recognized as the most important steel band competition in the world. Before the final on Carnival Saturday, preliminary competitions and semi-finals have taken place, so only around twelve bands remain in each category—small, medium, and large. The small bands have their final a few days earlier, so on Carnival Saturday the finals for medium and large bands take place. The event starts around seven o'clock in the evening and lasts until one or two in the morning on Sunday.

Carnival Saturday is also the children's day, when Kiddies Carnival takes place. One can see children from stroller-age to around seventeen years old in their costumes parading from a part of Port of Spain up to the Queen's Park Savannah and the stage where the judging takes place. I have always found the Kiddies Carnival one of the most exciting parts of the Carnival events.

J'ouvert, which comes from the French Patois for "daybreak" but can also have the double meaning of "I opened," is the official opening of Carnival. *J'ouvert* takes place before dawn on Carnival Monday, and participants parade and dance through the streets until the sun comes up. Some also cover themselves in grease, mud, or paint.

Before leaving Trinidad, we had to order our Carnival costume, which we then would pick up just before Carnival in February. Stanley had played Mas with a small band called Rabs Immortelle before; he knew the people, and we decided that band would be a good choice. We selected costumes of black and silver with headpieces that we would then use during the major parade of the bands on Carnival Tuesday. They would also provide us with a simpler type of top to be used on Carnival Monday.

February came fast. I had to go on a trip for UNICEF to India, so Stanley would leave one week before me so he could enjoy some of the pre-Carnival events, particularly listening to his favorite steel band, Renegades, practicing and fine-tuning what they were going to play for the Panorama finals. Renegades is one the oldest surviving steel bands, established in 1948. Their pan yard is on Charlotte Street in Port of Spain, very close to Oxford Street, and the Thomas family members had been in many ways involved with and supportive of Renegades for many years. Renegades had won the large band competition the year before, and the band was one of the favorites in 1990 as well.

I returned to New York from India on a Friday and was going to leave for Trinidad the following afternoon, Carnival Saturday, arriving at night. The flight from New Delhi to New York was around fourteen hours, and the time difference was ten and a half hours; I knew I would be tired, but I was still very much looking forward to the trip.

I arrived in Trinidad around eight o'clock at night, and by the time I was through immigration, had picked up my suitcases, and had made it through customs, it was close to nine o'clock. Stanley and his brother Simlon were waiting for me outside. They had already been up at Queens Park Savannah listening to some of the steel bands perform and were very eager to get back there in time to hear the Renegades. We had, however, a little time, and by the time we reached Port of Spain, we stopped to get some fried chicken and chips to take with us. The night would be long, and we would need something to eat.

We arrived at the Queens Park Savannah, with all its excitement, in time to hear Renegades playing—and they played fantastically. Even I, who was far from an expert, could here that. They played a tune called "Iron Man," which was composed by the well-known calypsonian Lord Kitchener, whose real name was Aldwyn Roberts. The crowd was excited, and so were we. Of course, we had to wait until all the bands had played and the results were announced. I had now the advantage of my jet lag: while others started to be tired, I was waking up! When the results were announced, we were all full of new excitement: Renegades had won.

The next day, Sunday, was a day to take it easy to prepare for the two days of Carnival.

I did not quite know what to expect.

First it was *J'ouvert*, the opening of Carnival, which started at four o'clock in the morning. We were there with Renegades, which was extra exciting since they had won the championship. I had never experienced anything like this, walking and jumping through the streets of Port of Spain to the sweet steel band music until after sunrise. Then we went home to get some rest and food before participating in Carnival Monday with our Mas band. Monday is the relaxed day, as some wear partial costumes, and some wear shorts and T-shirts. Stanley wanted us to try some special dance moves, and the bandleader of Rabs Immortelle liked it so much that he asked us to be in the front of our section doing the same dance moves on Carnival Tuesday.

Tuesday morning we were up early. Getting dressed in my costume and putting glitter on my face made me feel transformed into another person. Having always been very structured and disciplined, I felt suddenly freed up in a way I had never experienced before. It was fantastic! In the blasting sun, we "jumped up," doing our dance moves in front of our section when we crossed the stage in Queens Park Savannah. The tune that was played most that day, and which become the year's Road March, was called "We Ain't Going Home," which was perfect. We continued for hours through the streets of Port of Spain, so it was important to have good footwear, which we had. What an experience.

For most years until 2012, Stanley and I continued to play Mas with different and larger Carnival bands, including Barbarossa and TriniRevellers, but that first time in 1990 is still a wonderful memory.

From 1989 to 2004, we went to Trinidad twice a year, for Carnival and for my mother-in-law's birthday in November. Early 2001, we bought an apartment in Trinidad, and since I retired at the end of 2004, we have spent five to six months in Trinidad every year, divided in two periods of months.

Stanley and I have traveled throughout Trinidad over all of these years (and a few times to Tobago), from east to west and north to south, to see and experience as much as possible of this beautiful twin-island country.

9

Life Is a Mix of Sadness, Happiness, and Challenges

After Jim Grant passed away in early 1995, it was time to get a new executive director. The UN secretary general appoints the executive director of UNICEF after consulting with the UNICEF executive board. From the beginning, the executive directors of UNICEF have always been from the United States. As expected, the Europeans wanted to change that and came up with candidates. The United States had already submitted the candidature of Bill Foege, who had a lot of relevant experience. Then Belgium and Finland came up with candidates, both women, and the United Kingdom submitted the candidature of Richard Jolly, who was the deputy executive director of UNICEF programs. The UN secretary general, Boutros Boutros-Ghali, made it rather clear that he wanted the best possible candidate, and he wanted a woman. The Americans then withdrew their candidature of Bill Foege and instead submitted the candidature of Carol Bellamy, the director of the Peace Corps. She had also had three terms in the New York State Council, and she was the first woman to be elected president of the New York City Council, a position she held until her unsuccessful bid for mayor of New York in 1985. She also had many years of experience from Wall Street. After the necessary consultations, the UN secretary general appointed Carol Bellamy as executive director of UNICEF, and she joined the organization on May 1, 1995.

I had never had a woman as a boss before. I had always been, as a UNICEF driver called me, the "Boss Lady." It was a big adjustment. Carol, as she preferred to be called, and I also had different personalities. The first few months were difficult, but I did not give up. Gradually, things changed. We got used to each other, and Carol realized she could really count on me. Many difficult issues demanded attention.

During the last year of Jim Grant's executive directorship, with a strong demand from the executive board of UNICEF, a management consultancy company had performed a study of our management. The company made a number of recommendations, and it was up to UNICEF to work on their implementation. In addition, after an internal audit of the UNICEF office in Kenya, a number of mismanagement and misappropriations had surfaced, and I had the difficult task of informing Jim Grant that we had to dismiss the head of the office and a number of other staff members. It was particularly difficult since the head of the office was a staff member Jim Grant had always supported. An expanded audit was then underway to see what routines needed to change to prevent something like that from happening again.

Carol was strong when it came to management issues, which was an advantage during this period. She also gradually managed to gain the trust of the Executive Board, which made it easier to implement changes. In addition to the responsibilities I already had, she gave me more responsibilities, including the oversight of the UNICEF's Office of Emergency Programmes worldwide. I really enjoyed it, even though it meant more hard work, more travel, and longer work hours. For almost one year in 1999 to 2000, I was the only deputy executive director. When I asked Carol Bellamy to get an executive advisor to assist and travel with me, she said yes immediately. I received the most wonderful, hard-working, and experienced staffer of my choice.

My dad had serious health problems for many years, including two heart attacks and a stroke. He had so far always managed to bounce back, even though he was somewhat weaker every time. Stanley and I had gone to Norway to visit him and my mom and see the rest of the family at least twice a year. I had also taken opportunities to visit when I traveled to Europe or through Europe for meetings. I had always been close to my dad, and on every visit, whether he was at home or in the hospital, we talked a lot, about everything. In February 1997, while Stanley and I were in Trinidad, my dad fell at home and was again hospitalized. It had become clear to him and my mom that after this hospital stay he would have to go to a nursing home, as it was no longer possible for him to stay at home.

He seemed to do okay in the hospital, so there was no need for us to rush to Norway. We returned from Trinidad on February 18. On the morning of February 19, while I was dressing to go to work, the phone rang. It was my mother. She told me that the hospital had called to inform her that my dad had had a massive heart attack and had passed away. He was nine days short of 82. Even though it was not entirely unexpected, to lose a parent who has always been one's rock and supporter creates a lot of emotions, as well as a kind of empty feeling. We went to Norway for the funeral and spent a lot of time talking about my dad and his life. My mom, who was the same age as my dad and in reasonably good health, did very well. It was also great for us to know that my youngest brother, Morten, continued to live at home with her.

It was September 2001. The year had so far been hectic, with a lot of travel. Late in September, the United Nations Special Session on Children was going to take place to review what had happened during the ten years since the World Summit for Children had taken place, revise the goals that were set at that time, and link those goals to the Millennium Development Goals that had been adopted by United Nations member states in September 2000. While the Special Session on Children was a UN meeting, UNICEF was the substantive secretariat for the meeting and events linked to it. The good thing was that Carol Bellamy had appointed two additional deputy executive directors, so we had a full team at the top level again.

I was going to do one more trip before the Special Session on Children in order to attend a United Nations meeting in Geneva; I'd be leaving New York on September 10. Two days before, I was not feeling well. My doctor ordered me to stay home for a few days and not travel for the next month. I was not happy with the decision, but between the doctor and my husband, who were both concerned about me, I had no choice.

September 11 was a beautiful morning. I was still in bed, since I had promised to take it easy. Stanley had the day off and had gone to the Bronx to help one of his cousins with a car he had in his mother's garage. I had not even put on the TV; I had just been looking out the window at the blue skies and sun. Then the phone rang. It was Stanley asking me whether I had the TV on. He had just heard that a small plane had hit one of the towers of the World Trade Center. I immediately put the TV on, just in time to see the second plane hit the other tower. I was almost screaming out, "Stanley, that was not a small plane! It looks like a big passenger plane."

We all know what happened the rest of that day. We were under attack. Stanley managed to get home, and we were like everybody else, glued to the TV for the rest of the day and night.

At some stage I called UNICEF to check that everybody were okay, and while I was talking to Carol Bellamy, the towers started to crumble. None of us could believe what we saw.

The next day, I did not stay at home. I went to the office. Just arriving at Grand Central Terminal was eerie. A lot of heavily armed members of the National Guard were around the terminal. When I got out and started to walk toward UNICEF House and the UN, I could smell the smoke and burned material from the World Trade Center even though it was quite a distance away.

The staff had been excused from coming to the office that day, but a large number of staff members were there. Some had actually not been able to go home the previous day, since public transportation had been shut down for long periods and most of the bridges had been closed. They had been able to stay with friends, colleagues, or nearby family. I walked all the thirteen floors of UNICEF House and the premises we were renting outside UNICEF House to talk to staff. We were all traumatized, and unconfirmed rumors were reporting that the UN buildings were also terrorist targets. Everybody felt it both good and important just to talk and calm each other down.

One of the first things we needed to do was to formally postpone the Special Session on Children. The session was supposed to take place from September 19 to September 21. With all that had happened, there was just no choice; it could not take place as planned. At the first plenary session of the UN General Assembly, the Special Session on Children was postponed to early May 2002.

The US invaded Afghanistan early in October 2001 because they accused the country's Taliban government of sheltering Al-Qaeda leader Osama Bin Laden, who had masterminded the September 11 terrorist attack. They wanted to dismantle Al-Qaeda and deny it a safe base of operation in Afghanistan by removing the Taliban from power. After the fall of the Taliban regime, the Afghan Interim Administration was established at the end of December 2001, with Hamid Karzai as head of government. Elections took place in July 2002, and he became the president of Afghanistan.

Since she joined UNICEF as executive director, Carol Bellamy had had girls' education as one of her top priorities. In Afghanistan, girls had not been allowed to go to school under the Taliban regime. With the new government in place, she knew it was time to do anything possible to get children, both girls and boys, access to a quality education. The new school year in Afghanistan normally starts toward the end of March, and UNICEF was committed to supporting the interim government in its effort to open up learning to all children and to provide educational material to formal schools, home schools, and other learning environments through provincial education authorities. UNICEF also supported the interim government's social mobilization efforts to encourage children and teachers to come back to school when the school year started. Many teachers had been out of the classroom for up to six years, so teachers needed support in using the new learning materials that had been designed by Afghan educators. This was one of the biggest of UNICEF's undertakings there, particularly in terms of logistics.

UNICEF's office in Afghanistan had temporarily been moved to Pakistan when the US-led invasion had started in October. Gradually, the staff would now be moved back to Afghanistan.

Already having oversight responsibility of UNICEF's supply and logistic operations as well as its emergency operations, I wanted to see the Back to School Campaign and related activities as much as possible. It was impressive. A plant had been established in Peshawar, Pakistan, that provided more than forty thousand stationary kits to children. UNICEF also provided more than ten thousand of what we called "School-in-a-Box," each for up to eighty children. We also provided three million textbooks and eighteen thousand chalkboards. Hundreds of trucks were used to transport these materials from the plant in Peshawar to Kabul, Afghanistan, for distribution to centers around Afghanistan. In addition, more than twenty airlifts carried educational materials from UNICEF's supply division in Copenhagen. Additional materials would be distributed later in the year.

I wanted to go to Afghanistan as well. Unfortunately, because fighting was still underway, it was not yet safe for me to go to Kabul. Instead, relevant staff members at UNICEF suggested I go to Herāt.

Herāt is in the northwestern part of Afghanistan, and it is Afghanistan's third-largest city, with a population of around four hundred and fifty thousand. On January 8, the school bells rang for girls for the first time in six years. Within a week, fourteen thousand girls had registered, and by the time I arrived in mid-January, twenty-two thousand girls had registered. Classes were already being held in eight schools to assist girls with preparing for the start of the school year. Since the schools for girls had been closed for six years, many of these girls had never gone to school. I saw the excitement and joy they displayed when I visited some of the schools. I also heard what plans many of the girls had for themselves. Some wanted to be doctors, many wanted to be teachers, and I remember one who wanted to be an engineer. It was rewarding just to be there with them.

Back in New York, Stanley and I started discussing our retirement plans. Stanley, who would turn sixty on June 1, had already worked thirty-two years with Scandinavian Airlines. That meant he could retire with a full pension when he turned sixty. Working for an airline was even more stressful after September 11, so discussing he concluded, with my strong support and encouragement, that it would be a good option to retire. This would also give him the opportunity to spend some more time in Trinidad to see his mother, whose health had unfortunately started fail. The other benefit was that he now could join me on some of my trips.

Next was my turn. Working for the United Nations at the assistant secretary general level meant that I could not get a permanent contract; officials at my level only received short-term contracts for a maximum of five years at a time. My present contract was up at the end of 2002, and I knew that Carol Bellamy would most likely want to recommend renewal for another five years. The UN General Assembly had decided some years back that heads of UN agencies, such as UNICEF, could only be appointed for a maximum of two terms. That meant that she would leave as executive director of UNICEF at the end of April 2005. Continuing with UNICEF after Carol Bellamy left and having to transition with a new executive director was not what I wanted to do. So, I decided to tell Carol that when my contract was up at the end of 2002, I wanted it to be renewed only for two years, until the end of 2004, so I could retire a few months before her.

I have always been a well-organized advance planner. However, sometimes things happen that cannot be planned for, as happened to me in 2003.

Stanley and I had spent a wonderful time in Trinidad, enjoying Carnival and taking some vacation after Carnival. We had decided that he would stay in Trinidad longer than I would, both to have some work done in our apartment and to spend some additional time with his mother. I had to go on some trips for UNICEF, so Stanley would join me back in New York a week or so after my return from traveling.

I had returned from my trips and was attending a meeting with the UNICEF Staff Association. We had a lunch break, and some buffet-style food was served. The chairs in the meeting room had metal loop-style legs, and when I got up to get some lunch, I managed to get one foot tangled in one of the chair's loop legs and fell in an awkward way. After the fall, I could not get up by myself. Many people present helped get me back up in the chair, but I found myself in excruciating pain. I thought maybe an ice pack would help, but it did not, and I could not walk. There was no choice: an ambulance had to be called, and I was taken to the ER at New York Presbyterian Hospital. The chairperson of the Staff Association had already alerted a number of people, including my assistant, Elma, and she called me on my cell phone. I was in such pain, so I can only faintly remember what I said, but I vividly remember telling her not to call Stanley in Trinidad, as I was certain I would be home the next day. This time she did not do what I asked her to do, which was smart. She called Stanley in Trinidad, and Stanley's recollection was that she said that Mrs. Sham Poo had had an accident, was okay, but was right then in the hospital. Stanley was absolutely devastated. He called his sister and most likely some other family members and said he wanted to get back to New York immediately. One way or the other, he managed to get on a flight that would arrive in New York late that night. In the meantime, after arriving in the hospital and being examined by a doctor, I started to undergo a number of tests, including an MRI and a CAT scan. Two of the people who had been alerted about what had happened to me included Mike Corbett, the deputy director of human resources at UNICEF, who is a good friend, and Dr.

Sudershan Narula, who was the head of the medical department of the UN and another close friend. They both arrived at the hospital, as did my daughter, Elizabeth, all trying to help and all being very supportive. After a number of tests and x-rays, the doctor told me that I had three hairline fractures in my pelvic and pubic bones. I remember saying to myself, "Hairline fractures? That cannot be anything serious. I am sure I will be fine in a few days." Little did I know at the time that it would take months before I would be more or less okay. I was admitted to the hospital and moved from the ER to a regular room. Until the doctors were sure what was wrong with me, they had not wanted to give me any painkillers; now that I was allowed them and felt a little better, I still could not sleep. I had already been told that Stanley was on his way back to New York, so at a time by which I assumed he would have arrived, I tried to call him. It was wonderful and reassuring just to hear his voice when he answered. He was running to catch the last train to Scarsdale and told me he would call back as soon as he got home, which he did. The next morning he was in the hospital by my bed, and I felt better just from seeing him. I could still not walk, but with the help of nurses and Stanley, I managed to sit on the bedside. Stanley came to the hospital every day and stayed almost the whole day. It was a big achievement when I managed to get to the bathroom almost by myself with a walker. I realized after talking to the doctors that this would not be a quick fix. They recommended that I should be transferred to a rehabilitation center as soon as I had stabilized. After ten days in the hospital, I was transferred to Burke Rehabilitation Center in White Plains, which is not too far from where we live in Scarsdale. In addition to Burke being one of the best rehab centers, its proximity to home would also make it less stressful for Stanley to visit.

I had to do three hours of tough physical therapy exercises and training every day. After one week, I was able to walk with crutches instead of the walker, which was a big improvement. Since our house in Scarsdale is on three floors, I had to train on walking steps too, as well as do other activities, such as getting in and out of a car. During the whole period of therapy, I still had to take strong painkillers. For a person who rarely had taken a Tylenol, I was not too happy about that, but I was told that I needed the painkillers to be able to endure the exercises and therapy. After another week, I was able to use two canes instead of the crutches, and they were so happy with my progress that they told me that I could go home and then continue the physical therapy as an outpatient three times a week. I was also given an exercise program to do at home every day.

When one works in the UN system, one gets six weeks vacation a year. If one does not take all the vacation, one can accumulate up to twelve weeks vacation. Anything above that is lost if not used. I had already lost many, many weeks of vacation, since I had never had the time to take all of it. To avoid losing more, Stanley and I had already planned to take six weeks of vacation in Trinidad in 2003 and six weeks in 2004. The big question now was whether I would be allowed to travel. However, after three weeks of physical therapy as an outpatient, I was medically cleared to travel with instructions to do various exercises in the swimming pool at our apartment in Trinidad. After six weeks in Trinidad, under Stanley's strict care, I was back in good shape, walking well, and using only one cane occasionally, out of a sense of caution.

While I had been working a little from home before we left for Trinidad and had been on the phone a lot from Trinidad, I was finally ready to go back to work full-time. By then I had then been out for three months.

This whole unfortunate incident had taught me a lot. It had taught me about the body's fragility and how one never should take things for granted. It also made me appreciate the enormous support I had received from so many. Stanley was especially fantastic. He kept his eyes on me all the time, everywhere, and was so patient. The support I got from my daughter, Elizabeth, and granddaughter, Sonja, helped a lot too. And I could not have achieved being back in such good shape if it had not been for all the support of my UNICEF colleagues and friends as well. This experience also taught me not to rush so much and that certain things take longer than one thinks.

The rest of the year was relatively uneventful. While I started to travel again, I did curb it somewhat.

Then it was 2004, the year to say goodbye. The whole year was full of goodbyes; it was a very emotional year. Everywhere I traveled, a farewell party was arranged.

In early December, Carol Bellamy invited me to my official UNICEF farewell party. I am sure she received a lot of help planning it; however, the way she did it really touched me. Senior people from UNICEF and the rest of the UN system were invited, as were people from outside the UN whom I knew well. And on top of that, which was a big surprise, a video had been put together featuring pictures from my childhood; video clips of me from UNICEF; interviews with Stanley, Elizabeth, and Sonja; and greetings from two of UNICEF goodwill ambassadors, Roger Moore and Johan Olav Koss. I had had no idea that they had planned this, and Stanley, Elizabeth, and Sonja had not said a word about it.

My more than nineteen years at UNICEF, most of them as its deputy executive director, had come to an end. During these years, I had focused extensively on the internal administration and finances of UNICEF and had been able to do a lot to make improvements. But I had also traveled extensively. I had visited, as mentioned earlier, more than one hundred countries, many of them more than once. I had met with kings, queens, presidents, and prime ministers, but even more importantly, I had met and talked with ordinary people—in particular, women and children. I have listened to their fears and hopes, their realities and their dreams, and I hope that UNICEF's work will continue to make their lives better.

10

In a Slower Lane?

When one has worked full-time for more than forty-two years, one will always wonder what life after retirement will be like. For me, at least for the first six or seven years, life continued to be quite busy, but it moved at a slightly slower pace.

Before retiring, the UNICEF regional director for Latin America, knowing that I would spend a part of the year in Trinidad and Tobago, asked whether I would be interested in being the UNICEF special envoy to the Caribbean on a part-time basis. I thought that sounded interesting, and Carol Bellamy liked the idea too. She formally appointed me as UNICEF special envoy.

UNICEF had never had any real presence in Trinidad and Tobago. Since it was one of the richer countries in the Caribbean, very little financial support had been made available for activities there. Trinidad and Tobago had been a part of the eastern Caribbean area office in Barbados, but in 2004 UNICEF reassigned it to the UNICEF office in Guyana. Some additional funding was also made available, and UNICEF started to build up a small staff presence in Trinidad and Tobago, with offices in the UN building. In the past, I had always spent some of my vacation time trying to get more visibility and focus on UNICEF activities; I had been meeting with government officials in Trinidad and Tobago, including three different prime ministers, over the past fifteen years. UNICEF-supported activities in Trinidad and Tobago were a part of the programs of cooperation for Eastern Caribbean for 2003 to 2007 and focused on early childhood education, parenting support, HIV prevention in young people, and children's rights and protection.

Early in July 2005, we got a visit that we had been looking forward to so much: my granddaughter, Sonja, arrived. This was her first and, so far, only visit to Trinidad and Tobago. We had put together a program of activities that would interest us all. One of the highlights was the trip to Grande Riviere to see the leatherback turtles. I had never experienced this, and neither had Stanley.

Grande Riviere is at the North Coast of Trinidad, and it is quite a distance from where we live. It took us more than three hours to drive there, but it was more than worth it. We had booked rooms at a small beachfront hotel owned by a charming Italian. The leatherbacks come between March and September to lay their eggs. Two months later, the eggs hatch. We arrived at the perfect time to see the big leatherbacks coming ashore to lay their eggs, which they mostly do at night, as well as to see the small baby turtles emerge from eggs that had been laid two months earlier; the baby turtles dig themselves out of the sand and try to reach the open sea, usually early in the morning. We learned that leatherback turtles are the largest turtles on earth today and that some can reach up to seven feet long and weigh up to two thousand pounds.

Sonja decided to do the guided tour so she could see the big turtles coming ashore without disturbing them and also without disturbing the eggs that had not hatched yet. She told us how fantastic it was. We managed to see one big turtle ourselves; we watched how she laboriously dug her nest in the sand before laying and then covering the eggs over. She then slowly started her return to the sea.

While baby turtles normally dig themselves out early in the morning, some become confused by the light from the hotel's restaurant. Suddenly we saw a number of baby turtles around. Sonja and a few others tried to pick them up in small buckets to get them safely on their way to the sea.

Stanley was the first one to wake up early the next morning. He woke us up because he had started to see the baby turtles trying to dig themselves out of their nests. It was absolutely amazing. We would see the sand start to move, and then we'd see more and more of the small baby turtles digging themselves out and hustling, sometimes a little awkwardly, toward the open sea. Many of them do not survive to maturity, but we were told that the females that do will return to the same beaches where they were born to begin the cycle anew. Sonja, Stanley, and I were so grateful to have experienced this natural wonder.

Not long after Sonja had left, I headed on a trip to Panama, where the UNICEF regional office for Latin America and the Caribbean was located. I had promised the regional director, who was on vacation, that I would represent UNICEF at a summit of the heads of associated Caribbean states and governments in Panama City. UNICEF had been invited as an observer because of a side event on children with disabilities and because ending child hunger in the region was on the summit agenda. Arriving late at night in Panama City, I discovered that I had a message on my cell phone. To my surprise, it was the UN secretary general's office asking me to call as soon as possible. It was too late to call that night, so it had to wait until the morning. In the meantime, I was wondering and wondering what the call could be about.

I certainly found out the next morning when I called. I was asked whether I would be interested and willing to be the interim special representative of the UN secretary general for children and armed conflict; my rank would be at the undersecretary general level. The position had just become vacant, and it would be a few months before a more permanent replacement could be found. When I asked when it would start, I was told more or less immediately. While there were many other assignments I would have said no to, this one was tempting. Of course I needed to consult with Stanley before giving my answer. I called Stanley, who as always was supportive. I called the secretary general's office back and accepted the assignment until the end of the year. I also called the regional director for Latin America and the Caribbean and told him that he had to put my assignment as special envoy for UNICEF on hold until early the next year.

Upon returning to Trinidad, I made all the arrangements to return to New York and to working full-time for the next few months.

From my time in UNICEF, I was familiar with what had led to the establishment of the Office of the Special Representative for Children and Armed Conflicts as well as its current work. Based on recommendations from the Committee on the Rights of the Child and with strong support from UNICEF, the UN General Assembly, late in 1993, asked the UN secretary general to appoint an expert to conduct a study on the impact of armed conflicts on children. Graca Machel, who had been the first minister of education in Mozambique after its independence and an advocate for children's rights, was asked to undertake this challenging project, which she worked on for more than two years. She traveled to several of the countries affected by conflicts and met with a number of people, including children. She also met with a number of UNICEF staff members in these countries and had consultations at UNICEF headquarters, which is how I had the opportunity to meet her. I also met her later when I visited Mozambique. Graca Machel is the widow of both South African president Nelson Mandela and Mozambican president Samora Machel. The last time I met with both Graca Machel and President Mandela was in 2002 at the UN Special Session on Children.

Graca Machel's report had been presented to the UN General Assembly in 1996, which led to the decision to establish a special representative of the secretary general on children and armed conflicts.

I was met with a small but extremely dedicated office staff. I discovered fast that the office was underfunded, since a few positions were All costs, including staff costs, were funded from what are called "extra budgetary resources," which meant that all needed resources had to be raised from extra contributions by member states. I felt strongly that at least the core activities of the office, including the basic staffing, should be funded through the UN's regular budget. Having the advantage of knowing the UN system in and out, I managed to get a decision on that within my first two months in the office.

I also asked for an appointment with the new executive director of UNICEF, who had been appointed to that position in May 2005. The purpose of the visit was twofold. I wanted to reassure her that I was absolutely supportive of the fact that the special representative should not conduct operational activities or program development on the ground and that responsibilities should rest with UNICEF and other relevant parts of the UN that had the necessary mandates, field presence, experience, and capacities. I also told her that over the next months, I would position the office to focus even more clearly on its comparative advantages and added value. Then I asked her for a staff member from UNICEF to urgently fill the vacant post of executive officer. The meeting went well, and she assured me that I would get support. In less than two weeks, I had the person I wanted on board.

The 2005 World Summit, which in many ways was a follow-up and reaffirmation of the year 2000 Millennium Summit, was held at United Nations from September 14 to 16. One hundred and seventy heads of state and government participated. This was a unique opportunity for me to meet with as many government representatives as possible from the more than thirty countries where children's lives directly or indirectly were affected by armed conflicts. My focus was to solicit their support in doing whatever was possible to provide effective protection and relief to children in their own countries. It was a marathon of exciting, interesting, and sometimes difficult meetings, but I certainly managed to get my message through.

I left the office, as planned, at the end of the year, and I felt that the short time I had been there had enabled me, together with the dedicated staff, to strengthen the office and move this important agenda forward.

In the early part of 2006, Stanley's mother's health deteriorated further. We had already planned to go to Trinidad, but the day we were to travel a big snowstorm hit the New York area, and all the airports closed. We needed to get to Trinidad as fast as possible, and the airline tried to be helpful. We were able to travel to Miami the next afternoon, as soon as the airports in New York opened, and then catch an early-morning flight to Trinidad the next day. One of Stanley's nephews picked us up, and we went directly to the hospital. We were able to talk to my mother-in-law and tell her how much we loved her. We returned to the hospital again our second day in Trinidad, and we all felt that the end was close. She passed away early the next day, February 17, 2006. Stanley had lost a mother to whom he had always been close, and I had lost a mother-in-law I was privileged to have known.

During 2006, I continued to assist UNICEF in my capacity as special envoy to the Caribbean. I spent quite some time in the area office for the eastern Caribbean in Barbados, commuting back and forth between Barbados and Trinidad every weekend. Since the office in Barbados covered most of the Caribbean—apart from Guyana, Trinidad and Tobago, and Jamaica—this also gave me the opportunity to interact with people on most of the other islands, including government officials.

One trip that for many reasons was particularly interesting was one of my trips to Suriname. On this trip, Stanley joined me as well.

Suriname is the smallest country in South America, with a population of a little more than five hundred thousand. It is also considered a Caribbean country, and is a member of the Caribbean Community. It was previously a Dutch Colony and is the only independent country outside of Europe where the majority of the population speaks Dutch. There are, however, a number of local languages spoken in various parts of the country. Suriname has a number of ethnic groups, the largest being people of Indian descent and the second largest being Maroons; it was to an area where the Maroons lived that we were going. The Maroons are descendants of African slaves who fled the colonial forced labor plantations in Suriname and established independent communities in the interior rainforest. They have retained a distinctive identity based on their West African origins and speak their own distinctive languages. One of the UNICEF staff members with us on the trip came from a country in West Africa, and she was amazed that she could understand some of what the Maroons said when they used their local language.

The first part of the trip was by air. We left from the domestic airport in the capital, Paramaribo, on a local airline's Russian-built plane to fly into the interior of Suriname. In addition to UNICEF staff members and a few other passengers, the plane was filled with various types of cargo. Suriname has a large number of airstrips used by domestic airlines since flight is the only reasonably fast means of transporting food and other necessities to the interior of the country. Stanley, coming from the airline industry, had some concerns, to put it mildly, when we were to land. He was looking for an airport, but what he saw was an airstrip in the middle of nowhere. We landed, however, safely, without any problems.

Our first stop was a school. During their lunch break, the kids ate flatbread made from cassava with homemade peanut butter, which was both good and nutritious.

Our trip then continued on the river. We all got onboard a motorized longboat, which was indeed really long. We traveled for around two hours to reach our destination. The river was full of rocks, so sometimes we had to travel slowly, and one person was always in the front to look out for the rocks.

The house where we were going to spend the night belonged to one of UNICEF's counterparts who stayed in the capital during the week. The house had only one bed, which had to be assembled, and everybody decided that since Stanley and I were the oldest, we would sleep in the bed. The rest of our UNICEF team had to sleep in hammocks.

We were to have met with the *granman*, the head chief of the village, but since he apparently was very old and not doing too well, we met with the *kapitein* instead, who is more the day-to-day chief of the village. We took a tour of the village, and after we had had something to eat, we met with a lot of young people. One of the main discussions was how to prevent the spread of HIV/AIDS. The young people were outspoken, and we had a fruitful discussion and interaction.

The next day we returned the same way we had arrived, by longboat and plane. Stanley, who had never been on a trip like this, was particularly happy to be safely back in Paramaribo—though he really had enjoyed the trip and found it exciting.

Over the next few years, until the end of 2010, I continued to participate in key meetings for UNICEF in the Caribbean and assist in other ways when needed. I enjoyed it very much, and it also allowed me to gradually ease myself into retirement.

Stanley and I continued to visit my mother in Oslo regularly. Late December 2005, Elizabeth, Sonja, Stanley, and I went to Oslo to celebrate my mother's ninetieth birthday. She was still doing quite well for her age. Unfortunately, a few months later, she had to have part of one of her legs amputated. For a long time she'd had a sore on her leg that would not heal due to poor circulation. The doctors had tried everything, but in the end they had no other choice than amputation. While she recovered remarkably well, her health continued to be a challenge. Thanks to the combination of in-home helpers and the fact that my caring youngest brother, Morten, lived at home, she managed to stay at home. In early 2009, however, it was clear that she needed more care, and she moved to a nursing home. The nursing home staff was very helpful, and it was reassuring for me that I could get updates from them on how my mother was doing from across the miles, in addition to the updates I received from my brothers.

Stanley and I had planned to go to Oslo in late June/early July. However, based on the nursing home's updates, we decided to go a little bit earlier. We arrived in Oslo on June 22, and that afternoon we went to see my mother. She was happy to see us and seemed fairly spunky. We went again the next day and even took her out in the wheelchair to the beautiful garden surrounding the nursing home. The following day, things changed. She did not want to get up and did not eat much. This continued for the next two days, and it became clear to us—Stanley, my brothers, and me—that my mother was not interested in fighting anymore. The nursing home staff continued to make her as comfortable as possible. When we arrived on June 26, she was asleep. I have seen people after they have passed away, but neither Stanley nor I had seen a person dying. We experienced that that day. We were there when my mother took her last breaths. She took one breath, which I thought was the last one, then one more, and that was it. It was a peaceful end to a long life.

There are so many thoughts that go through your mind in a situation like this. Your mother is gone. While all the memories persist, she is no longer there. I am now the oldest person in my family; my two brothers and all my cousins are younger than I am. I am now the oldest generation.

I have often thought that my mother was just waiting for me, that she wanted to see me once more, and then she knew it was okay to go.

For the last eight years, I have certainly been in a much slower lane. I do not feel old, but I enjoy doing things at a slower pace. For most of my life, I got up early and went to bed late. Now I do not have to do that. I can still get up early and go to bed late if I want to, but I do not have to do it. Stanley and I have time to enjoy life and each other. We can go see a movie or to a jazz concert or do many other things just when we feel like it, not thinking so much about the time anymore.

Now is the time to reflect on what an exciting life I have had and all I have been able to achieve.

While writing this book, I have skimmed many pieces of paper that I have kept over the years, mostly to refresh my memory. I enjoyed reading many of the pieces, such as speeches I have made. I've decided to end this book with a quote from a speech I made to an Asian and Pacific ministerial conference in 1994:

> I would like to close on a personal note. I have been
> involved in struggles for women's rights and gender equity

since the early 1960s. I am grateful that I as a girl had the opportunities that permit me to be here today. But still, so many do not have these opportunities. So much potential is lost to stereotypes, discrimination, or neglect.

My experience has taught me that seeking equal opportunities does not necessarily mean the pursuit of identical roles for men and women. I would be the last to conjure up stereotypes—we've had enough of those. But I do believe that there are qualities that women have in abundance that need not—must not—be lost in the struggle for equality and equity. That is why it is important that we have a fair distribution of women decision makers at all levels of society, from grassroots levels to the highest levels, in politics and in the corporate world. I am convinced that women have a special contribution to make to society and that the world will be a better place when all women are fully empowered to make it.

A Note on Sources

This book is extensively based on my own memory and, when it comes to my very early years, stories and information I got from my parents. I have also used information from speeches I made, my notes, my trip reports, and other briefing notes.

Apart from the names of close relatives and friends, all names mentioned belong to people who are already in the public domain.

None of the banks where I worked in Oslo, Norway, are still in existence. They were either merged with or bought up by other banks more than thirty years ago.

About my years working for UNICEF, I have also checked a wide array of material, including internal and external UNICEF reports; official UNICEF board papers and decisions; the official UNICEF website; UNICEF's annual publication, *The State of the World's Children*; and UNICEF annual reports. While I have not quoted any of them directly, Maggie Black's 1996 book *Children First: The Story of UNICEF, Past and Present*, and Adam Fifield's 2015 book, *A Mighty Purpose: How Jim Grant Sold the World on Saving Its Children*, have been good background material and have also helped refresh my memory.

Printed in the United States
By Bookmasters